ALL THE
GLORY
GOES TO
GOD

A TRUE STORY

MICHELLE STRONG

ISBN 979-8-88616-226-4 (paperback)
ISBN 979-8-88832-393-9 (hardcover)
ISBN 979-8-88616-227-1 (digital)

Christian Faith Publishing
832 Park Avenue
Meadville, PA 16335
www.christianfaithpublishing.com

Printed in the United States of America

CONTENTS

A NOTE FROM
THE AUTHOR

When I was a little girl, I grew madly in love with the Lord. I would sing His praises profoundly, at the same time engulfed in His presence. I would be running outside, feeling the warmth of the sun on my face, in my bare feet, leaping over the rugged grass. A wild flower would be growing here and there. I long to reproduce the memories that my mind holds so close to my heart for they are exuberant and pure of the Lord. My voice was off-key as I sang loudly in worship, swirling in His heavenly sunlight.

I plopped down in the sweet-smelling, long grass, and as I listened to the crickets' chirp, one jumped on my knee and then off again. There was nowhere else my heart desired to be. Looking over to my father's garden, it had grown immensely. Out of the corner of my eye, I saw a leaf break free from a tree branch that was ready to create space for new growth, but my five-year-old self had yet to comprehend the correlation. As I watched the wind tenderly move the leaf through the air, gliding slowly toward the ground, I felt like the leaf. Different from the rest, not connected, and incomplete. I was too awkwardly tall to be five years old, and I never quite fit in anywhere. At the time, I could not see that I was connected to it…to the more expansive comprehension that God was the tree, and He was preparing me prophetically for the space He was creating for my growth.

My thoughts were interrupted when I heard my mother calling for me. I wanted to stay hidden in the tall grass and sing songs to the Lord, but Mother had other plans for me and my four sisters with school starting next week. I got up and started running toward the house, not knowing my life was about to drastically change. In the days to come, the days that the Lord had ordained for me, I would be lying in a hospital bed as the doctors would be preparing my parents for the process of my contingent death.

This is a piece of literature written about how God revealed to me the secrets of Heaven that He had intended for me to know. I did not access the mysteries of the Spirit until I was traveling through my adult life, and He brought to my recollection the journey I went on while lying in that hospital bed. It was a night in the month of January during the year 2020 that He sent me a dream where He brought me back to the encounters I had in my five-year-old body. He sustained me while I slept in a coma and guided me to remembrance of the moments I spent in His protection while my spirit was disconnected from my earthly body. God has shown me the immense, unconditional love He has for all of us, no matter our age or race. *He loves us to the core of our beings.* It is in this place that He is teaching me how to use the gifts the Holy Spirit intended for us to utilize. It is about giving *All the Glory to God*. When the Holy Spirit chooses to help others through the power of dreams and visions, gifts of healing, working of miracles, wisdom, knowledge, and faith, it is our responsibility to respond with yes and amen. Just as His promises are to us.

This story begins with me as a little girl playing the game Kick the Can one night in my backyard, only to find the message the Lord was speaking to me through this moment on my journey. The symbolism between being caught in "jail" in a game is no different from me barring myself from the "freedom" the heavenly Father has for me. I have been praying for you who has picked up this book, for I know that His calling for you is beyond what you could ever fathom. I pray the Lord guides your heart and mind to be postured with an eagerness to learn all that He has written for you throughout your adventure called life.

I will sing of the Lord's great love forever; with my mouth I will make your faithfulness known through all generations.
—Psalm 89:1 NIV

CHAPTER 1

Deliverance

*You are my hiding place; you will protect me
from trouble and surround me with
songs of deliverance.*
—Psalm 32:7 NIV

I can feel my toes squishing against my sweaty rubber sandals as I ran in the tall grass that lightly sliced across my legs. Giggling as my sister Vicki, seven, and I, five, tried to hide from the others. The can had been kicked and was sailing through the air, freeing one of the neighborhood boys. We had to outrun my fourteen-year-old sister, Mary, who was fast…*really fast*. At this point, I was not sure how many others she had caught, and if we ran deep enough behind the garden, I knew of a safe hiding place.

It was a late summer evening in August: the year 1976, dark, hot, and humid. My long hair would have been sticking to my face and neck, but earlier that day, my oldest sister, Kiki, sixteen, thought it was a clever idea to cut my hair.

She appeared to be having trouble keeping the sides straight and kept snapping at me. "Michelle! Sit still!"

We were on the back stoop of our house, and all I wanted to do was go play. I was doing everything but sitting still.

"Michelle! I told you, you must hold still!"

I did not care. I just wanted to go run.

Then my mother pulled in from the grocery store and right into the garage that was detached from the house. She got out and went around to the trunk to grab the bag of groceries. Looking up, she saw us on the stoop. Long clumps of hair laid on the ground while Kiki was still holding the scissors in her hand. Boy, Mom was mad. She started screaming so loud. But that was nothing new for our house. We did not think much of it. I still just wanted to go run and play, but she was truly giving Kiki a hard time.

"Kiki, how could you do this? She is going to kindergarten next week!"

I ran in the house and looked in the mirror. Well, *I* was delighted!

I started to skip around, saying, "I look like Peter Pan, I look like Peter Pan!"

Mom continued to yell, and Kiki tried to defend her actions, explaining she had been trying to make the haircut even.

Sliding now into the dirt behind the garden, moonlight shone a path for us to see clearly where to hide. Sweat dripped down my hairline, relieved that my long hair was no longer sticking to my face and neck. I could hear the can clanging out into the grass, wondering who had just been released from "jail," sneaking back around to the side of the garage to see if they just experienced "freedom."

Just then, my mother came out the back door and yelled for my sister Vicki and myself to come in for the night.

Ugh! I thought.

I was covered in dirt, *usually am*, for I spent most of my time outside. For that is where my heart felt the freest, away from the chaos of my family life. I could hear the other kids still outside my bedroom window while my ten-year-old sister, Rose, just kicked the can, yelling out to set the others free.

Before we took a bath, Vicki and I counted how many mosquito bites we had suffered. There were so many, we lost count. Feeling uncomfortable from wanting to scratch all the bites, I sank into the hot bathtub. After the bath, we put on our jammies, and my mom tucked us in for the night—but not before we said our prayers.

*Our Father in heaven, hallowed be your
name, your kingdom come,
your will be done on earth as it is in heaven.*

—Matthew 6:9–10 NIV

CHAPTER 2

Enlightenment

My eyes were so heavy, and it was hard to breathe. I was able to open my eyes ever so slightly, and I saw a nurse standing over me with a needle in her hand, realizing I was lying in a hospital bed.

Panic was racing through my mind, and I started pleading with her, "I want my mommy!"

As I looked into the nurse's soft bluish-green eyes, she gently smiled at me. I cannot remember what happened to me. When I fell asleep, I had been tucked in for the night, but now, I was in a hospital and in excruciating pain. Where was my mom? What happened? How did I get this ill? I looked around and fought back tears.

I eventually understood that I was terribly ill and had just awakened from a coma after five days. My mom and dad tried to explain to me what had happened, but they were speaking in big words. Words that were beyond what my five-year-old brain could comprehend: encephalitis, meningitis, and pneumonia. I didn't know what they mean. They were telling me I was extremely sick because I slept a long time where they couldn't talk to me, but they were also relieved and happy to see me.

Seeing the doctor then entering, he sat down next to me. He kindly explained that there are mosquitoes that carry viruses that can cause illnesses in human bodies. I apparently was bitten by a mosquito that was carrying a disease. These certain viruses were making my little brain swell from the encephalitis, and the protective membranes covering the cerebrum were inflamed from meningitis. The doctor was translating the scientific understanding of my diagnosis into the capacity to a five-year-old. He went on to explain how he followed the protocol of a procedure known as lumbar puncture. This course of action removes fluid out of the spine and communicates from patient to doctor what the next steps needed are. Continued to decode the acquaintance I currently had with pneumonia in relevance as to why I couldn't breathe. His description was simple: My lungs had air sacs filled with fluid infecting them. I was trying with all my might to keep my eyes open and breathe in a full breath of air. As this was happening, the doctor explained because of the severity of my pneumonia that I was specifically struggling with breathing, and as I heard him continue to speak, I fell back asleep.

Weeks have passed before I had finally got to go home from the hospital, and my family seemed as if nothing in our world had changed. My sisters were angsty to go shopping, Dad seemed to be making something related to canning tomatoes, and Vicki had utterly convinced me that I had missed Christmas. All was well in the household, but it was a temporary comfort. I was still noticeably sick. My mom and dad rushed me back to the hospital, and it was not long before we had discovered that I now had hepatitis.

The Lord your God is with you, the Mighty Warrior who saves. He will take great delight in you; in his love he will no longer rebuke you, but will rejoice over you with singing.
—Zephaniah 3:17 NIV

CHAPTER 3

The Dream

Looking over, the clock read 4:10 a.m., January 20, 2020. My husband was trying to comfort me, but my tears were flowing, which were sinking into my pillow, and I now felt the moistness against my neck. I did not know where or what had happened when God sustained me forty-three years ago when I was only five, but through all the glory of God, He revealed to me the mysteries of this part of my journey. This place was introduced to me in a heavenly dream:

I was standing in an empty room with my sister Kiki and my now-grown daughter, Julia. As I leaned my ear into their conversation, I heard Julia chuckling something about me as a child. Stepping over toward them, Julia was standing to the right of her aunt Kiki, while Kiki was holding a few photographs in her hand. I looked over Kiki's left shoulder, and I realized that the photos were from when I was a child. I examined one of the pictures in Kiki's hand with a closer intention.

My heart sank to my stomach, and I gasp. "I knew it! I knew that happened! Where did you get those pictures?" I asked.

As my brain processed the correlation of events I experienced throughout my journey in this life, shock arose within my body. I had the understanding that I was five years old in the pictures she was holding. My hair was all chopped up from cutting it off when we were little girls, and in this photo, I had on an olive-green angel dress. It was here that I was smiling immensely, and I could feel the joy of the Lord, invading every part of me.

Suddenly, the dream transitioned...

My viewpoint was from the tippy-top corner inside a twenty-thousand-foot industrial warehouse, and I had an exquisite bird's-eye view of the whole place. The sunlight was beaming in through big checker block windows directly across from me, illuminating every inch of the space with His heavenly glow. The warehouse was active with children, all ages and all races, who are laughing in harmony. A few adults, *were they angels without wings?* watched over the children who were playing happily. Some of the children were to the right of the establishment, and they were jumping rope while others were sitting on the floor, playing board games. As I observed my surroundings, I noticed two of the children were playing checkers as the sound of loud talking and laughter filled the air.

Above all, I noticed the atmosphere. I could feel it radiating to the core of my being... An overwhelming sense of

God's love was bursting out and pouring over all of us. *A magnitude of love.*

Over by the windows, a large industrial side door swung open, and roaring laughter permeated the room as a marching parade of children appeared. The leader of the parade was a girl wearing an olive-green angel dress, just like I was in the photo. Her ensemble was a green lace embroidered top that has a soft flowing mesh skirt with angel wings fluttering. This little girl carried a long pole including a purple banner while skipping. The boys and girls behind her were in a procession, their knees moving high and low in front of them. Each child held various ribbons of all different colors, twirling them aloft in their hands, as they are yelling and laughing with delight. I was astonished and in awe. *I wondered if I was seeing correctly.*

In an instant, I was floating over my five-year old self, and it seemed like I watched her for quite a while, even though it was only for a few moments. I could see myself so clearly. My hair was cut short. My arms and legs were their gangly selves. *It was me.* I was getting to watch myself being so happy, like I had never been. What was happening in this place was like something I had never experienced before. Children's love for each other was undefinable; they already knew each other's souls and saw their shining light. God was guiding us to be who He called us to be: pure light, pure joy, and pure happiness.

Instantly, I was wide awake, lying in my bed at 4:10 a.m., with tears running down my face. I knew God just revealed a whole new part of His creation to me.

This little girl, with an awkward appearance, was *loved* and loved beyond what I had ever fathomed or understood for me. It is hard for my adult self to imagine, let alone believe, that God could love me. I did not even think my own earthly father was very fond of me. All I could feel was an incredible, magnificent, and unconditional love beyond anything I had experienced in this life. Yet in this dream—was it a dream?—the whole room was filled with love, and one did not even question it. It was the most beautiful sound you had ever heard, as if you could feel it flowing through your hair, caressing your fingertips, and moving across every part of your being like a symphony from heaven. The children were engulfed in it, and there was no room for pain or for anger, only God's heavenly love.

> *"And God will wipe away every tear from their eyes; there shall be no more death, nor sorrow, nor crying. There shall be no more pain, for the former things have passed away,"* *Then He sat on the throne said,* *"Behold, I make all things new."* *And He said to me,* *"Write, for these words are true and faithful."* *(Revelation 21:4–5 NKJV)*

I knew God had been intentional with me and sent me a divine appointment. My life would never be the same. Forever changed. God gave me a glimpse into something I had been missing my whole life. Maybe it has been there but just out of my reach. It was like something deep inside of me that I always longed for but never have felt worthy to receive for myself.

I felt so incomplete before I even entered the hospital room at five years old. My outsides did not match my insides. I was anything "*but*" a cute little kid, and the world around me let me know it. My internal soul was carefree and never found concern about what I looked like because my liberation was to be outdoors to run and play without restrictions, and in so doing, I found freedom within God's grace.

The place God sustained me while I slept in a coma and now brought me back to this night at age forty-eight astounded me. It opened a part of my being that I didn't know existed, and it communicated a unique kind of intimacy in this world. *From heaven to earth.* It seemed impossible that the overflowing love I felt with the other children in this warehouse could be attainable in this life. No one cared what you looked like. We knew each other's souls and saw our shining light. Until I had that dream revealed to me, I could not discover this deep and pure joy. It was then, awaking at 4:10 a.m., that I saw the beauty, seeing the space where God had placed me to sustain my existence while I slept during the coma at five years old. I believe that there is an unconditional love that has always been obtainable to human beings…if I could only embrace what God has been intending for me.

Growing up, I had always been very sickly child. As a result, I felt like I never fit in anywhere. In my household, my father's love was conditional on my actions. If I got the grades in school he was expecting of me, then all was well, and was rewarded with love and acceptance. If my behavior lived up to what he felt it should be, I received the love I longed for; otherwise, I would be considered insignificant. It left me feeling very unlovable and incomplete. Not having many friends, I found myself additionally feeling deeply insecure. Walking through my young years in search of someone who I would fit in with, I never had the realization of the abundance and magnitude of love that God wanted to give to me. When the heavenly Father took me back and showed me where He sustained me throughout the coma, I perceived that all the children perfectly loved each other, we were unified. Every one of us was friends, and our joy for each other was insurmountable. The presence of God's love was all around us and embraced us with a feeling of safety and security. The feeling saturated the room.

I believe God wanted me to write this book for other moms, dads, or loved ones that are in turmoil over one who is sick or unreachable in their lives. This was a place I waited as a child to find out if I would go back to my body or if my soul was to travel on to heaven. I do believe that God wanted me to let others know He loves His children, and they are in a safe place, wrapped in His heavenly arms, even when we can't communicate with them lying in a hospital bed. Seeing myself in this photograph as I was in this heavenly space, I knew I was not only safe but also complete. I was happy, *immensely happy*, for I knew exactly who I was in the Lord even in all my incompleteness. I feel the Holy Spirit is guiding me to speak a message: to give you peace in your trials and pain.

And so we know and rely on the love God has for us. God is love. Whoever lives in love lives in God, and God in them.
　　　　　　　　　　　　　　　　　—1 John 4:16 NIV

CHAPTER 4

Separation

To fully understand the impact God revealed to me, I must first take you back ten years to see the mess I was making of my life. I always believed in a God of one's own understanding; however, on this day, my viewpoint of Jesus changed.

*****

As I paced the kitchen floor, gripping the phone tight in my hand, I responded, "Is there any time available today for the doctor to see Steven? I just know something is wrong." I explained to the receptionist at the pediatrician's office…

While Steven, my son, and I sat in the examination room, the pediatrician explained to me that I needed to take my son to the emergency room.

Is he that sick? I thought to myself.

My head was spinning, and all I saw was fear on Steven's face. The doctor informed me that we must go *now* because Steven had type 1 diabetes and his levels were skyrocketing. I did not understand what that meant.

Steven looked at me. "Am I going to die?" he asked.

"No, of course not," I told him, looking into his big brown eyes.

In my heart, I did not know, and I was doing everything I could to hold back the flood of tears that were about to break loose.

Looking at the calendar on the wall in the pediatrician's office, it reads September 5, 2011. I realized that Steven really had not been acting right this entire weekend. He kept complaining how thirsty he was, and he could not drink enough, an unquenchable thirst. When Steven first sat on the examination table at the pediatrician's office, his doctor went over all the basic questions and had then decided to do a finger blood test. Coming back into the room after the blood had been pricked from his finger, she explained the results revealed that his blood sugar levels were over the monitor's capacity. A normal person's blood sugar levels range between 80 to 125. The pediatrician's monitor only went up to 500. Knowing this information, she went on to clarify the urgency of the situation and why we needed to go to the emergency room immediately. She stressed the point that "Steven has type 1 diabetes, also known as juvenile diabetes, and the blood sugar levels were alarmingly high." As I stepped out into the hallway, I could feel my heart pounding. I called my husband, David, Steven's stepfather.

"Do not leave," David told me.

"Wait for me. I will be right there and go with you to the emergency room."

Arriving at the emergency room, I did not know what to expect. Everything seemed like it was happening in slow motion, and anxiety was grabbing a hold of me. I watched my eleven-year-old son go through a series of tests. Finally, we were getting settled in the hospital room, as I watched the nurse *once again* inject a needle of insulin into him. I was trying to comprehend what the nurse was telling me.

"Check Steven's levels before he eats and decipher whether his levels are high or low. Depending on the number provided by the glucose monitor, you can make the determination over how much insulin to inject. He will have to receive injections each time he eats a meal."

An injection every time he ate a meal? What? I don't think I am understanding this whole thing correctly. I was trying to go over this repeatedly again in my mind.

As I kept attempting to process this last portion of information, she was now explaining to me the other element of being a type 1 diabetic. To find out about Steven's sugar levels, he would need to do a finger prick first.

Wait, I am supposed to get him to do this before he eats a meal or other times throughout the day? I can't even get him to eat a vegetable.

My brain was swirling. My little boy looked overwhelmed and exhausted. Bob, Steven's dad, rushed in his hospital room and sat beside him on the bed. He tried to cheer him up while I step out into the hallway with my loving husband and Steven's stepdad, David. He wrapped me up in his arms. I let him know that it was okay to go home because Steven had to be admitted for three days, and the hospital was allowing me to stay with him. Entering back into Steven's room, I saw his father got him to smile. A moment of relief on Steven's face.

Wearied from the day, Steven fell asleep. Over in the corner the nurse pointed to a royal blue, stiff-as-a-rock couch that she said I was allowed to sleep on. *Really that is what I am sleeping on?* Looking at it with a sigh, yet beyond worn out from the day to care, I lay down and was just glad the hospital let me stay in the same room for the night. I snuggled into the antiseptic-smelling pillow to find myself not able to sleep. Instead, I was angry, beyond angry.

How could You let this happen to my little boy, God? What kind of God are you that would do this to a child, let alone diagnoses like cancer and all the other kinds of illness?" In my head I was screaming at God.

A feeling of disappointment was washing over me, heart-wrecked, questioning everything I had thought about Jesus. I thought it was God who had been there guiding me when I went through so many hard times in my life. I must be mistaken for I would never let this happen to my little boy. *So why would You?* It felt like God just pulled the rug out from under my feet.

I awoke to the sound of the nurse checking Steven's vitals, and I had the realization in that moment that my depression was consuming me. I had been treating it with medication for some time. Watching him sleep and not knowing what was ahead for him on his own journey, my anxiety equally was spiking. It felt like my lungs were being sat on by an elephant. I got up and headed into the bathroom to splash some water on my face.

Fear was rushing through my body, and I was telling myself I need to hold it together. *We've got this!* repeating it in the mirror over and over again.

Our family is very high-spirited. We love each other through it all and find ourselves laughing often. I am not a yeller, and I have the tendency to want to make everyone around me feel happy. I think this might be why I get down on myself in my moments for I have the fear I am always failing at helping others.

Will I be able to step up and do what needs to be done? Will I be able to figure out how to give him the correct amount of insulin? I thought as I watched a drop of water drip down my face.

My faith was crashing down all around me as I watched the impact of this disease affect Steven's whole life, with school, with friends, and especially sports. Having the awareness that he was going to have to inject insulin correctly throughout the day to keep himself alive and knowing this was part of his walk for the rest of his life was heartbreaking. It wasn't like I made a conscious decision to swear off God. I just stopped talking to Him all together. Distancing myself from Him. I questioned His existence, and in so doing, I discounted the power of faith.

I am the vine; you are the branches. If you remain in me and I in you, you will bear much fruit; apart from me you can do nothing.
—John 15:5 NIV

CHAPTER 5

Seed

Time has gone by quickly, and three years have passed since I found out Steven has diabetes. While I thought of removing God from my life would not make a difference, many things have started to spiral out of control. I am struggling with my own depression, and I feel like I am in a deep, dark hole that I am trying to claw my way out of. The anxiety keeps growing. I am so stressed and worried, and those around me are feeling the impact.

Watching the neighbor boy jump the fence, bounding through the sliding back door into the kitchen, I checked the time and realized we were going to be late for me to drive them to high school. My daughter hadn't come downstairs yet when suddenly I stopped dead in my tracks. Whipping my head around and looking at the neighbor boy with eyes wide for we both knew instantly that smell, ruminating down the stairs into the kitchen: strong and potent, for there was know other smell like it. He looked at me with shock, yet knowing that I, too, already knew what the smell was…weed! Just then, my daughter walked into the kitchen. She was looking at us with a blank expression on her face, like "I am ready to go, let's go." I turned and ascended the stairs with great force, taking two steps at a time. My foot had not even landed on the top step, not needing to go any farther, but I could not seem to stop myself. My body had taken over itself and was proceeding to go into her room where it hit me, an overwhelming smell of marijuana.

I tried to calmly walk back down the stairs, telling myself to take a deep breath, *Breathe in, breathe out, in, out.* I was ready to scream at the top of my lungs, but I knew that would not help the situation. My head was orbiting in every direction.

What has happened that got us to this point? I was thinking to myself. Not sure how I was supposed to be reacting.

Telling them to get into the car, I started lecturing Julia and the neighbor boy as I drove them to school. That was when she dropped the next bombshell on me. She was telling me she was done with public school and was going to drop out. That did it. I threw the breathing technique right out the window.

Screaming at her now, I said, "You have one of the top-grade points in the high school!"

Fury was raging.

Looking over at her sitting in the car seat next to me, I thought, *Why am I wasting my breath when she is stoned.*

Pulling back into the garage, sitting in my car, I thought, *What has gone wrong? I have increased my medicine. I have read books on "how to experience true joy in life," like what is up with that! I am tired. I am tired all the time. I want to run away, but where? My life is spiraling out of control, and my depression and anxiety are affecting others.*

At this point, my son no longer attended regular public school and was attending online school because his anxiety had worsened. Thinking back to when I was a teenager, I did not exactly walk a straight line in high school. I caused my parents much grief and heartache throughout my adolescent years which I could not acknowledge at that time. The thing was, I did not realize I created pain and heartache for myself by not listening to my parents' guidance. Depression and anxiety had already started setting in during my teenage years.

As I was sitting in my car, processing my past, a momentary flash went through my mind about God. *Where was God during those years?*

It was here that I realized, in the course of those years, I had put Him on a shelf.

I did not have the fight in me to fight with Julia, so when I picked her up from school, I asked if we could talk. She reluctantly agreed. I tried to understand what had changed about the public school because she just started a new year. She explained that she was just miserable. The school building, because it was new, equated to a prison. The kids were mean, and the teachers cared but only to the extent of the bare minimum. *Not* in the capacity that was needed to handle this abundance of teenagers on a daily basis. They were concerned with their students' learning of the curriculum but not as individual humans. So on that note, I told her that if I was miserable at my job, I would look for another job and provide the suggestion that maybe she could go and shadow some of the private high schools around us. Not having much reaction to this suggestion, we got home, and she went up to her room. She had to decide for herself, but I did not want to lose her down a rabbit hole just because I was emotionally lost.

I remembered that last week, my sister Rose mentioned to me that her nephew, Max, just started at the local Lutheran High School and how much he was loving it there. I thought that might be a great fit for Julia being a boys/girls school. Going up to her room, I knocked on her bedroom door. I decided not to wait for an answer. I just walked in. She was in bed, depressed and moody. I told her about Max and how much he was truly liking Lutheran High. She wanted nothing to do with it, angry that I would even bring it up. I went downstairs, exhausted from her reaction, feeling the chill of the cool fall evening, I decided it was a perfect night to put a fire in the fireplace. Going out to the sunporch, I brought in some logs, setting them down on the hearth. I resolved after great debate within myself, to call Max's mom and see how she liked the Lutheran High School, and if so, if she thought Max would give Julia a call. Curling up on the couch and listening to the crackling wood in the background while talking to Max's mom, she could not say enough glorious things about the school and how happy Max was there. She said she would ask Maxs if he would be willing to call Julia. It must have gone well because, within days, she asked me if she could shadow Max at the Lutheran High School.

My feet throbbed looking up at the clock and realizing half of my workday wasn't even up yet. Hearing my cell phone ringing in the back room, I inconsiderately turned from the customer and raced to grab the phone luckily just in time before it went to voicemail. A counselor from Lutheran High School wanted me to meet with him at the end of Julia's school day where she was shadowing her cousin, Max, and I agreed. Walking into the building at the Lutheran High School, there seemed to be something different, and I was trying to put my finger on it. But I cannot seem to be able to. The counselor was finishing showing me around the building when the dismissal bell rang. Julia was leaping down the hall toward me, and her face was glowing.

I thought to myself, *When was the last time I saw that look on her face?*

She was then right up by my side. The students filled the hallway, but there was a different spirit in the air. I could feel it all around me. She was pleading with me, I could hardly hear her over all the laughter. Yes, that was it. Laughter. They were happy. She wanted to go here. I told her we would talk about it, but in my heart, I already knew I would make it work. I had no idea how I would pay for it, but I would make it work.

It did not take long once she started at the Lutheran High School to see a change in her. She jumped into the curriculum with both feet. Listening as she told me about reaching an understanding of a truly loving God, I still had my doubts. The bars of captivity were strong around myself. Now she was growing leaps and bounds in her own personal faith. My eyes could not help to see what was happening right in front of me. My daughter who was going through hard growing teen pains was finding this confidence, acknowledging that it was coming from the Lord. I would be lying if I didn't say it opened my eyes a teensy bit and made me want to investigate what was making her life lighter and happier. This was the first time in three years I considered looking into the true God. My daughter planted a seed.

The new year rolled around, and a customer came into the shop where I worked. She was blissfully happy and sat down in my chair. She was excited because it was a new year, and she has made a New Year's resolution. Not missing a beat, she went on to explain that she had chosen a word to help her grow. Okay, now she had my attention. She continued to explain how you choose a word and be mindful of it (such as peace, joy, or freedom) the entire year. She suggested discovering the word as it was used, everywhere—on pillows, in stories, or on book covers. So I decided to pick a word. Why not? I saw how happy Julia had been. I was going to see if I could just get a little faith back and see if I could believe in Him again. This seemed a little risky for my trust had been considerably wounded by Steven getting diabetes. I chose the word *believe*. Wondering if I could really believe in this God that Julia kept talking about.

This seemed crazy. I should have started counting how many times I saw the word *believe*. Since it appeared to be everywhere. I just walked past a building in larger letters than myself, and on the side of it was the word BELIEVE. Is God really calling to me, or am I just making this up in my head? But it almost seemed impossible that the word *believe* could be innumerable places.

I turned around and walked back to the building, stopping, and looking at the word *believe* once more. Inside my body, there was a longing, almost a feeling of pulling me toward the Lord, telling me, *I am here. I never left you.*

But my brain just did not trust it. I was climbing out of a long dark hole of despair and, yes, disbelief in a God that I feared might be a punishing God.

I planted, Apollos watered, but God was causing the growth. So then neither the one who plants nor the one who waters is anything, but God who causes the growth.
—First Corinthians 3:6–7 NAS

CHAPTER 6

Surrender

Growth has been slow. Even though I now believe there is a God, I am not creating any space for Him to have reigned in my life. Still wanting to have control over all the situations happening around me, I flew down to my daughter's Bible college in Lakeland, Florida. It was the end of her sophomore year, and we were packing up her things to bring home.

As I rolled over, my body ached. I was getting too old to sleep in a bunk bed. I heard my cell phone ringing. The clock read 1:36 a.m., and the phone was just out of my reach, lying on top of her desk. I stumbled out of the bottom bunk, reaching for the phone, and realized I did not recognize the number. Leaving the phone on the desk, I decided while I was already up that I would sneak down the hall to the bathroom. Coming back to her dorm room, I noticed there was a voice mail notification on my phone.

Usually, I would not pay any attention to this, but something was nagging at me. I picked up the phone and clicked on the notification, and while listening, I let out a shriek. My son, Steven, was telling me in the voice mail that he had been arrested. His voice was trying to sound brave, but I could hear fear in his undertones. He continued to tell me that he and a buddy were sitting in a car on the side of a road, smoking a joint after curfew. Now I could hear him trying to be strong and not cry. Once again, my heart was breaking. It was the end of his senior year in high school, and he was on the varsity baseball team. I burst out into tears, my daughter was trying to get a grip on what I was telling her. Suddenly, I became aware that she was rejoicing. I could not help but look at her like she was nuts. She was literally jumping around her dorm room, giving praise to God, while I was sobbing. Still confused and frustrated by her acceptance of God's intervention, I started to make phone calls because I realized that with the one phone call that Steven was allowed to make, he chose to call me. We were in Florida, and I now needed to be back to Cleveland.

Things just continued to spiral in my life. He was such a good kid. I could not figure out what I kept doing wrong, and I was questioning everything I had done as a mother. I always thought all you have to do is love your children and everything else will fall into place. But as the years have gone by, I know *now* that there is so much more to it than that. Nothing my kids ever do will ever make me stop loving them. I wonder now if there was a way I could have guided them differently that they wouldn't have to go down some of these rough roads.

The flight was long and frustrating. I pulled into the garage and rushed in the door of the house to see Steven standing in the kitchen. The look of devastation was on his face. I was not sure what to do. Should I hug him? Should I yell at him? My heart was breaking into a thousand pieces, knowing he just spent the night in jail. Steven went on to tell me the story of what happened the night before and followed with what the consequences of his actions might be. Then the look on his face became really distorted for he just received a call from his baseball coach, and he had been removed from the team. When joining the high school team, he signed a contract that had a portion of its composition incorporate a statement about finding a player in the position of being arrested. If one was, for any reason, found guilty or not, they were instantly let go from the team. Steven had worked extremely hard to be on the varsity baseball team. This was the first year he made varsity, and it was his senior year. I went to him and wrapped my arms around him and told him I was just glad he was home and safe and that we would figure this out, but with that, I must ground him from the car for a week. He did not fight me on this. He seemed to totally understand.

Two days passed, and my heart was so heavy for him. Not knowing what was going to happen with the whole court system. The lawyer suggested an outpatient treatment program which he was willing to do, but watching him seem so lost after departing from his pitching position on the baseball team, I knew it was punishment in itself. I went to the lower level where he was playing video games and told him he was not grounded from the car anymore.

I was not mad at him, not at all, but that I was scared for him…truly scared of what might happen with him having to go to court. All this was enough punishment.

Now reflecting, I think about how the Father might look at things differently when I make choices that are not good for me. When He sees me hurt and my heart is aching, I think He does not want to punish me, and I think about this situation with my son. Maybe the Lord is like me. He is scared for me and what my earthly consequences might be for my behavior. Just like me wrapping my son up in my arms, the heavenly Father would want to engulf me in His love and wrap me in His arms.

I called my doctor for many months had passed since this situation with my son and my anxiety was through the roof, hoping she could get me in right away. I was seeking a change or increase in my medicine for my anxiety. Something has to help, right? *Maybe if I was just on the right medication.* I had been drastically searching for joy and true happiness for I had this ache inside myself that I could not figure out how to fill. Despair was consuming me for I did not see any hope, like a dark hole of helplessness within my soul.

God knew how to get my attention, how He needed to intervene, and how to guide me into understanding that it was not I who had control. He knew one area in my life where I could not run from him, when I slept…dreaming:

In a tunnel, darkness all around me, way off in the distance, a light was shining through a curve-shaped doorway. As I walked toward the light, darkness encompassed me, but as I continued to walk closer to the lighted doorway, it kept getting smaller. I could see what looked like a prairie through the doorway now, even though the doorway was still a ways off. I picked up my speed because the doorway continued to get smaller.

I hesitated for a moment, thinking to myself, *I wish David could go with me?*

Suddenly, I saw a giraffe on the other side where the light was coming through the curve-shaped doorway.

A long and eloquent giraffe, her face pierced at me, like trying to say, "Are you coming or what?"

Deciding then to go, I picked up my speed and went through the doorway. I started soaring over the land, like a bird in the sky. As I soared, I went over the green lands that resembled skinny blades of rich grass dancing like waves brilliantly in the sea. Over hills and tops of mountains that reflected illuminating spheres of white snow, the sunlight bounced a sphere of light off the top. Trees were beneath me, and their leaves were flowing like a musical instrument and then soaring over a desert that was infused with sparkles, making the earth beneath a field of gold. It was stunningly beautiful, and I was free, I could breathe. For the first time in so long, I could breathe.

Immediately, I was wide awake in the middle of the night, listening to my husband gently breathing, lying next to me with his head on the pillow. Thinking about this incredible dream, I was aware of the feelings rooted in this moment of my journey for the dream left me longing for more. I could not figure out what the dream meant or what I had just experienced for that matter. It was beautiful and freeing, knowing this was the most vivid dream I ever experienced in my life. Somehow, I knew it was from God, beyond this dimension of transparency, but I had no idea what He could possibly be communicating with me.

Conscience of being outside for too long, for my hands felt frozen, even threw my thick winter gloves. I pulled one off to catch a snowflake in my hand, watching as it melts, the ice-cold winter breeze whipped across my face. A feeling of deep sadness consumes me as I set the shovel down in the garage after shoveling the driveway.

I thought to myself, *What could that dream mean a few days ago?*

Deciding then to go plop down in the snow, I watched big snowflakes fall all around me. The stillness in the air was certainly peaceful. Even though I felt still hollow inside, I knew there had to be something more fulfilling to this life. What was God trying to get through to me when I had been in the tunnel, plus everything I encountered while soaring, surely something? The dream was remarkably vivid. The snow started to accumulate on top of me as I thought about how Julia, after Christmas, decided to take a semester off college and was attending a local church. She kept asking me to attend church with her, but I held her and the thought of church at arm's length. I had done the church thing. It just was not for me.

Several months had passed, and it was a late evening at the place I worked. Things were continuing to stay the same in my life, even after that unbelievable dream. I felt as if I would never come to understand the significance of what God was referring to me throughout the dream. Saying goodbye to my last customer, I closed the door and locked it. Heading to the little breakroom in the back, I stopped and sat down on the folding chair.

Placing my face in my hands, I thought to myself, *Done. I am done. I am done with worrying about my job, my finances, and my parents' health, and I am* SICK *of being anxious all the time.* Now vocally exclaiming, "God, what the hell?" I screamed at Him, "I am so sick of all this! Why doesn't anything ever change?"

Experiencing feelings of desperation, madness, and overwhelming waves of sadness, I dropped to my knees. I was crying out, as tears were running down my face.

"Please help me, Lord!"

My heart was raw, and I longed to have my connection back with Him. I was truly beaten down, surrendering fully, pleading for help. All at once, I found this stillness within myself. It felt like God placed His right hand on me for I was no longer frantic, but calm, peaceful. A peace washed over me.

Getting home from work, I ran up to my daughter's room. I knew that my daughter's faith had grown to a new understanding of abundance in trust of the Lord as she had unconditionally dedicated herself to Him. Explaining what just happened at work and the peace that washed over me, I prayed that she would have some input on my encounter. She had been showing me a different viewpoint of the Bible, a way I had never looked at Jesus before. It was from a loving perspective, one that was not of a punishing God but a truly loving God.

Julia's face lighted up, and her eyes looked like they were dancing for she went on to say, "Mom, I have been praying for this a long time, since I have been in high school that you would find the Lord. He loves you so much and wants to be your friend. He has never left you."

She grabbed me then and wrapped her arms around me. I felt joy rushing through my body. I had a fleeting moment of the love the Lord must have in store for me. Once again, she extended a hand to go with her to church, and this time I went…

It was a sunny, pleasant Sunday morning in April 2019. The church was in an auditorium, and they had all the lights turned off. Only the stage was lit up. Worship had just started, and the music was excessively loud.

I thought to myself, *I tried this once before.*

Julia was in high school and was attending a different church than the one my feet were standing in today but this type of church nonetheless. At that progression of my journey to faith, five years ago, I beelined for the door. Not really my type of church, being raised Catholic, but this time, I promised myself I truly would try it out and not leave. God had been pretty vigilant with pursuing me, and I needed to figure out what He was telling me. I needed to be willing to pursue Him back.

People around me were raising their hands and praising while singing. The music was pounding through my body. Julia was next to me, vibrantly praising away. All this was happening in the atmosphere around me, while I was hoping I was not in some type of cult. The pastor got up and started to preach, different from any priest that I had ever heard. There was no coincidence that God had a plan to have me here, in this moment of time, for God was talking right through the pastor and directly to me. God was speaking over me exactly what I needed to hear, pulling apart my soul piece by piece, yet radiating so much of His love and mercy unto me. It did not take long for my tears to start flowing. I recognized that I had a lot of work ahead of me if I wanted to breathe again. *In any capacity.* I had new confidence rooted in my soul that I was going to make it there…to the understanding of freedom I had in the dream where I was flying over the mountain tops. There was a way to find an answer, and it was with the Lord. I didn't know how yet. It was just a feeling. Searching now and this church opened a door.

> *Ask, and it will be given to you; seek, and you will find; knock, and it will be opened to you. For everyone who asks receives, and he who seeks finds, and to him who knocks it will be opened. (Matthew 7:7–8 NKJV)*

Breathing in the smell of the aroma of my coffee while watching the sunrise on my screened-in back porch. The light was breaking through the cracks within me. Lifting the anxiety and occasions of depression that I didn't realize had pulled me down to great depths, I was coexisting with chemical imbalances that were starting to overtake me. Lately I can actually feel the lightness of me being able to breathe again. A season of my life has gone by, and as I allow God in more, I see Him working all around me. Before, I had been locked in, not understanding there was an illuminating light. I am realizing there are people around me who love me, who have been close to me, and in fact have been longing to reach out and help me the whole time. Crawling out of the hole I had dug myself into took a lot of people who had been showing me faith, love, and a lot of patience. Sipping my coffee, I started to feel the glow of the warm rising sun. I propped my feet up onto the couch, while I watched a robin tug at something out in the grass, I had a deeper revelation of the love God showed me through it all; He was behind the scenes the whole time. He has been placing all these amazing people around me to guide me through my ups and downs. Setting my cup of coffee down on the side table, I could hear David on the phone in the other room. How this man did not give up on me? I have no idea, loving me unconditionally through all of life's hills and valleys.

Fear not, for I am with you; Be not dismayed, for I am your God. I will strengthen you, Yes, I will help you, I will uphold you with My righteous right hand.
—Isaiah 41:10 NKJV

CHAPTER 7

Fear No Evil

As I continued to walk through my days, this surprisingly exquisite dream stayed in the forefront of my mind.

While putting away the dishes, I asked Julia, "Remember that dream I told you about when I was walking in a tunnel? I was wondering do you think God could have sent it? Because my mind can't stop thinking about it, and what would He possibly be telling me? Is He calling me to do something?" I turned around in the kitchen and looked over at my daughter as she was closing the refrigerator door.

She smiled gently, reassuring me that I was not that different, saying, "All this has been written before. Others have prophesied."

"What?" tones of disbelief in my voice. "When? Where?" with eyebrows raised.

She said bluntly, "Mom, read the Bible. Daniel had dreams, Joseph too, and many others."

I was shocked by this. Growing up as a Catholic, I knew many biblical stories; however, I never read the Bible. This sounded very intriguing to me.

One might assume that I would have gone running through the house, looking for where I placed our Bible, thinking I'd jump in with both feet, wanting to start reading the Bible right away after Julia told me this exciting news. Not exactly. However, I did look up and read the book of Daniel and read about Joseph (Genesis 39–41), understanding others' prophecies a little bit better and trying hard to figure out what the Lord was saying to me in my captivating dream. I thought it might be a good idea to join a Bible study class. Going to the church's website, I saw they were starting one very soon. Even the thought of going to this class made my anxiety rise, so I asked Julia to go with me to the Bible study, for they were held at church members' homes. She graciously agreed.

It was a cool, dark fall evening as Julia and I walked toward their home for Bible study, inhaling the woodburning of someone's logs in a firepit, while hearing the crisp, dry leaves under my feet. We entered their home, and the scent of vanilla filled the air. Beautiful lit candles were all around. I could hear laughter in the back of the house, coming from the kitchen. My daughter and I went around to the back. Seven young adults were sitting around, drinking cocoa and cider. Julia seemed to know everybody; however, I knew no one. My first instinct was to run, feeling totally out of place.

I thought to myself, *All these young people know about the Bible, and I know nothing. I am going to sound like an idiot.*

They got up, and we went and sat down in the living room. I told myself to take a deep breath and try to open my mind. As I listened to others talk and share, I was intrigued about the Bible. I needed to stay put. This was just going to take time. At the end of the night, I felt like I opened a new door of fellowship and adventure into understanding and the Bible a little bit more.

Not long after starting to attend this Bible study, God one night revealed His second most astonishing dream to me. The last dream this vivid happened nine months ago, and this one threw me for a loop:

I was in the house where I grew up. The kitchen and the dining room were in the back of the little ranch home, and in the front was the living room. The evening was approaching, and I looked out the back screen door to see the clouds were an ominous granite gray. The setting sun upon the cloud tops was the only brightness left in the day, and the trees joined in the unfolding threat. I felt a surge of fear run through my body. There was a window over the sink that looked out into the backyard. Vicki, my sister, was standing to the left of the sink, drying dishes, and the back door was to the right. My two girlfriends, Alyson and Irene, were in the living room, including Julia, my daughter, who was sitting on the couch in the living room. Julia was crying, holding a tissue in her hand. My one girlfriend, Irene, was trying to get to her car in the driveway, but we somehow knew something was not safe outside. We were waiting for the right opportunity for Irene to go to her car. I looked out the back screen door to see when it would be safe for her to run to the car. Back and forth, I went from the kitchen door, through the dining room to the living room. This time, coming back from the living room and walking into the kitchen, I caught my sister Vicki's eye while she was drying the dishes. Her face has an expression like she was analyzing the situation. I once again hastily went from the back door through the dining room and into the living room where the three of them were waiting.

It finally seemed safe, and I told Irene, "Now, go now, quickly."

And she ran out the door down the steps. As I watched her just barely making it to her car, I went back and checked on the others in the living room and told them Irene made it. The two looked relieved, but they were still upset about something. I went back to the screen door, looking out into the impending woods. My instincts were on alert. I noticed a shadow way back in the yard. I heard a strange howling sound, and then I saw it. It had long legs and an extended nose, growling, snarling, and foaming at the mouth with his eyes dark and wild. I knew right away it was a wolf, over-proportionate in size. He was a distance off but was moving toward me quickly. It looked like something you would see in a *Harry Potter* movie. I immediately looked to my left, and there was another, and now another huge long-legged gray wolf to my right.

I started to count the wolves, "One, two, three, four, five, six."

As I counted, each one was crossing the yard at greater speed almost to the house, and they were moving in on me. Instantly, the wolves formed two straight lines, but now there were many of them coming straight up the back-steps right at me. The wolves I noticed at this point had a chained harness around their neck, which caused them to be jolted back right before they reach me behind the back screen door. Their eyes were wild, and their mouths drooling at me. Three more inches and they would be through the screen and have eaten me whole. Right then, a woman was standing next to the over-proportionate, snarling wolves. The toughest woman I had ever seen, with a smirk on her face…cruel, immoral to the core, and ready to kill. Her face was rugged like she had been doing this for a long time. She was wearing army camouflage and was holding a semiautomatic rifle. She pulled back on some kind of lever on the rifle, and it made a noise.

My mind just snapped, and I looked right at her and started screaming at the top of my lungs, "GET OUT! GET OUT NOW!"

I continued to scream when my husband woke me up. I was shaking all over. This was the second most vivid dream God had ever sent me. In the first one, I could breathe, flying over beautiful landscapes. In this dream, I was scared to death as if it was right out of a horror film. But in the second one, my beloved family and friends were at risk with me. I shared the dream with a trusted handful of people, asking if they knew what it could mean. No one seemed to be able to interpret what the Lord was trying to warn me about. I felt it in my gut that something bad was going to happen, and I could not shake the feeling. Someone from the Bible study group pointed me in the direction of someone who wrote a book about prophetic dreams because the author had a dream about 9/11 before it happened. I looked down at the date on my cell phone. Yesterday's date was October 3, 2019. It helped me feel not as isolated, knowing that someone else has had dreams like these. Still, I knew something was coming, although I could not discern what, or with clarity, and I surely did not know how to stop it.

Yea, though I walk through the valley of the shadow of death, I will fear no evil; For You are with me; Your rod and Your staff, they comfort me. You prepare a table before me in the presence of my enemies; You anoint my head with oil; My cup runs over.
—Psalm 23:4–5 NKJV

CHAPTER 8

Heavenly Love

November arrived with blustery winds. The Lord kept showing up in remarkable ways, and I could see Him stirring in my life. Surrendering my world and ways to Him, I thought things would go more smoothly. This just had not been the case. For today, my earthly father was dying. I had been watching the situation take a toll on my sisters this past year and noticed the exhaustion on all their faces, as my dad deteriorated in front of us.

My head was lying on his chest. He was barely breathing. I watched his eyes flutter, and his mouth slightly moving. I knew he was talking to someone not of this world but of the heavenly one to come. As I could feel every bone of his ribs on my face, he was a skeleton of a man now. His face gaunt, lined, and haggard. A tear rolled down my cheek.

It was hard to imagine my life without my earthly father. We had a very difficult walk together. Years before his *now* passing, I came to peace and acceptance within myself over my dad. I had the realization that he did the best he could with what he was brought up knowing. I looked over at my mom, sitting in her big brown chair with her face crumbling, lost in her personal grief. The pain transformed her, considering how long she had loved this man to now being separated from him for the first time… must be incredibly painful. I walked over to her, kissing the top of her head. Telling her that I was right here and that I loved her.

I thought to myself, *I wish somehow I could lighten her suffering.*

My husband was being gentle with me as I was trying to rush the kids out the door to the car so we were not late for the funeral home. I could see the agony in my children's eyes because of their closeness to Papa. It had been a long year, and the whole family was feeling depleted.

The day was finally over, exhausted and still freezing. This was a record-breaking cold day for November. A feeling of gratitude to finally be in my bed, I pulled the covers over my head, searching to find relief from the cold. All I longed to do was sleep away my emotional exhaustion; however, the heavenly Father had other plans for me. While I slept, He was showing up for me and letting me know He would never leave me. Through all of God's glory, He was reaching out to me through this lovely connection of a dream…

I found myself back in the little ranch house where I grew up as a child, standing in the kitchen with my husband. We were so excited because we were going to a celebration. He had just finished baking and decorating a beautiful three-layer white frosted cake. The kitchen was in the back of the house, and the back door was open. As brilliant light was coming through the screen door from the setting sun, filled with magnificent orange and pink clouds vibrantly rich as if painted on the sky. I held the box steady while David put the cake in the box. He was finishing cleaning up the kitchen when I turned and skipped down the hallway and passed the bedrooms. I continued to go out the front door and down the steps. The steps were along the front of the house, and I happily skipped down them. When I abruptly stopped before I got to the last step, I detected a change in the air, almost as if it was thicker. Continuing, my feet reached the driveway, and I turned to look to the right toward the street. Seeing all the big evergreen trees hanging low, lining the driveway that had been planted there when I was a kid growing up, was reminding me of a time passed. Then I looked to the left up the driveway where the sun was setting so beautifully that it captured my breath. Taking note of the basketball hoop where I played as a child, I also observed three posts running along the driveway where my father would have held flowers up on. I looked closer and saw a little adorable stuffed animal of a crow tied to each of the posts. The second stuffed crow looked at me and smiled, giving a little wave of her wing.

I thought to myself, *I must remind my sister, Mary, we need to take those down as we are getting ready to sell their house.*

Then I looked up the driveway toward the garage, which was detached from the house, and there, to my surprise, was my father standing. Everything about him was soft and gentle. His eyes sparkled. Seeing no worry lines that used to go across his face as if they had vanished. Beautiful and healthy with a glow radiating to create his final form. He smiled at me and blew me a kiss. The setting sun was so orange and fantastically pink behind him. Then he was gone. All I could do was sit down, right there, in the driveway, and started to cry and cry really hard. My clothes had all turned white as I continued to cry. I was sobbing so hard in my dream that I was crying in real life, and my husband tenderly woke me up.

I was transformed by such a revelation that God spoke to me in this loving dream. A beautiful heaven that my earthly father was now entering to be pure; safe, without pain; young again; and in a healthy body.

My father was saying to me, *Don't worry. All is well with my soul.*

And he said to him, "Truly, I say to you, today you will be with me in paradise." (Luke 23:43 ESV)

God showed me something in this dream that I hold very close to my heart. Realizing once again that the heavenly Father needs me to share with others that there is a splendid, undeniable place we get to go to after this world. That I belong not of this world but of the next. My goal is not to try to achieve riches on this earth but to show others the beauty of the heavenly Father and what love He has given me. Peace and comfort, grace, and mercy.

CHAPTER 9

In the Forest

Two months after the dream about my earthly father, God revealed to me the experience where He sustained my existence as I slept during my coma at age five. God was shaking me awake. I could not figure out what was going on with me and these profound dreams, but I was ready to start investigating what He was calling me to do, realizing everything that I thought was important in my life was not. I needed to readjust my way of thinking and what I was living for. The Lord took me to a place that gave confirmation of unconditional love, where His heavenly love surrounded me. God's love was so powerful and so dramatic that it literally shook me awake. I had been missing this aspect of my life. My depression and anxiety had pulled me under countless times. I didn't see there was a true Savior walking beside me. I realized now I needed to reach out to the Father to find this place of deep heavenly love, which

I experienced in a coma. I understood that it was not of this world. I also believed I could attain His unconditional love in this life. I was blocking it, shutting myself out from His grace. I recognized now that He wanted to give these gifts of freedom to all who encompass this earth, appreciating the thought that the Lord wanted me to share in this moment with others, but how do I break these chains, which have held me down?

The euphoria only lasted a few days after God revealed to me where He placed me while I slept in a coma. That intense love, that heavenly love, was slipping through my fingers. At this moment, being aware of what the heavenly Lord showed me, I feel like I have spent a life imprisoned in my own personal jail, trapped by my shame and guilt, causing me to emotionally run away. I am still carrying this heavy load. It is not so different from when I was a child playing Kick the Can, caught in the jail, waiting for the mercy and grace of the Father who comes and sets me free, only for me to run and hide from the Lord once more, instead of running to Him. I continue to put the heaviness on myself, trapped in time and space, losing time in my life by not carrying out the dreams that He meant for me all along. Right now, I want to find my true calling. I wonder if I have been missing the mark.

My nights continue to be restless for God in all His diligence continues to send me more and more dreams, wondering what my husband must think of me for I am not even sure what to make of it myself. The only one who seems to understand is my daughter, Julia.

God throws me another curve ball. My head is tumbling in the confusion of what, in all His heavenly glory, could be telling me through this dream. How can I help His people if I cannot understand?

Nighttime had fallen. I was in the driveway where I grew up, standing close to the garage, which was detached from the house, and the outside garage light was on. I heard a rumble in the air. Turning, lifting my eyes to the dark evening sky, I saw a streak of lightning.

I thought to myself, *I love storms.*

When I heard giggling, it startled me. I instantly turned and looked to my left. The house was behind me, and the garage was in front of me with a driveway in between. Out a bit further from the driveway was the yard. A little girl, around three years old, was riding a red tricycle through the grass. Even though darkness had fallen all around us, I could see her from the glow of the outside house light. She was giggling and giggling, riding her red tricycle toward the house. Yet behind her, right in a row, were two over-proportionate wolves. I knew immediately, even in the state of dreaming, that these were the same wolves from the last horrific encounter. With their long legs, extended noses, and dark eyes, they were tiptoeing behind her. The wolves were not growling or snarling, not trying to catch her. At least not yet. Fear ran through my body. Seeing a light on in the kitchen, I started running toward the house, up the backsteps, throwing open the back door. When I got to the door and opened it, I tripped and fell flat down. Looking up to my right was my sister Vicki, standing in the kitchen by the sink, drying dishes.

I hollered to her, "The wolves are out there again! They're back!"

My husband woke me up for I was frantic! Frantically screaming. He was trying to calm me down, but I was freaking out and simultaneously telling him this dream.

While I blurted out questions at him, "Why didn't I run to the little girl and save her? What are these very vivid dreams about? What am I supposed to do about these things?"

In my head, I was going over and over the past series of events. The first dream about the wolves was in October. At this moment, it was the end of January 2020. I pondered who I can turn to help me with uncovering the interpretations of these vivid dreams, trying hard to connect what God was trying to tell me. My insides were unnerved. Everything inside of me was proclaiming SOS and telling me something was coming. I tried not to overreact in front of others because I did not want them to think I had totally lost my mind.

Within a few weeks, I heard about this crazy virus coming out of China called the coronavirus. Shock was not only sweeping the nations but through my body. My head was rushing with thoughts, looking back and wondering if this had been what God was revealing to me in these dreams—the prophecy of the spread of the coronavirus. The wolves each represent a continent, one to seven. The many wolves in a straight line on a chained harness being the seventh continent or North America, including the United States. The first wolf was initially so far away (China perhaps?), and each one became closer until the seventh, North America, which hit the United States, where I live, especially hard. The woman, who I believe is the disease itself, was right there at my door, ready to take people out and to kill as many as she wants to and still wants.

Is this what God has been trying to tell me the whole time? Has God been telling me that this horrendous virus was coming and that I needed to do something? But what? What could I possibly do? I am a nobody to the governing functions of this world, and I would not even know what direction to guide people in if you paid me. I did not see this coming, and I had just heard on the news that it does not seem to be affecting children the same way as it does adults.

I could feel my anxiety starting to rise inside of me, and I rushed to the phone, calling the woman I work with, Julie, and asked her, "Have you watched the news since you got home?"

Julie said, "Yes, I was turning on the news channel when I heard they did determine the effects on children are less likely for them to become severely ill. Once I heard this I thought of your dreams with the wolves that have been troubling you. When you think about it the little girl is on a tricycle, the wolves are close, within reach but not trying to catch her."

I felt despair growing within me, unsettled by this new information, which I was pondering if God had been revealing this to me the complete time. I took a breath before I ask her, "Do you think God was using the dreams regarding the wolves to show me about this virus?"

Hearing the alarm in her voice over this unexplained terrifying virus, she said, "My friends have had dreams that have come into fulfillment, sometimes it took many years.

You felt something was on the way, and you did not know what or how to stop it."

That was when I acknowledged the weight of importance that God was guiding me to have an understanding with Him through these dreams. That God wanted me to take this virus seriously and listen, taking the precautions needed to protect myself and others around me the best I can.

Each of you should use whatever gift you have received to serve others, as faithful stewards of God's grace in its various forms. If anyone speaks, they should do so as one who speaks the very words of God. If anyone serves, they should do so with the strength God provides, so that in all things God may be praised through Jesus Christ. To him be the glory and the power for ever and ever. Amen.

—1 Peter 4:10–11 NIV

CHAPTER 10

Direct My Path

My dreams seem so intense. I disclosed the occurrences of this part of me to few I cherish enough. All the same, one is my best friend, Alyson. We have walked a long road together, and she knows every aspect of my life. Second is my husband, trusting him with every bit of my being. Thirdly, my coworker, Julie, for she walks in the light of the Lord and is always in the quest of Him. Fourthly, but never last, is my fantastic daughter, Julia, who loves Jesus more than anyone I have ever met. I pray that those four do not think that I have totally lost my mind for I am feeling so alone. I knew that there must be others with the gift of prophecy from the Holy Spirit, but where? I asked Julia if she knew of others, and she felt there was, suggesting I talk with a woman at our church named Victoria.

After service on Sunday, I went up to Victoria and introduced myself. I thought I must look like a deer in headlights and figured she would for sure think I was off my rocker. I am not sure at this point if I was physically shaking or if that was just happening inside my body. Part of me was embarrassed. Is that the right word? I felt moved and honored that God has chosen to speak to me in these very intimate dreams; however, who in the world would believe me? I am not sure that if someone else shared dreams like these with me, I would necessarily believe them. It has an "off the wall" sound to it.

Victoria listened intently and reassured me about my dreams from the Lord. Guiding me with her own experience, she led me to an understanding of how God might be speaking to me. She suggested that I keep a dream journal and pray to the Holy Spirit for guidance to reveal His purpose. Victoria also went on to suggest that I get a Christian book about understanding your dreams and visions. She said the book helped her with having guidance and clarity of her dreams.

I went right home and ordered the book on Amazon. That night before I tucked in, I put a notebook and pen on my nightstand. Waking up, the clock read 3:21 a.m. I wrote a few things down that I was dreaming about and fell back to sleep. Hearing the alarm go off at six-thirty in the morning, I reached over to my husband and insinuated that he hit snooze. Starting to fall back to sleep, I remembered writing down some things on my notepad during the night. Eager to see exactly what I wrote, I swung out of bed. My feet touched the cushiony carpet as I grabbed my notepad and snuck into the bathroom, trying hard not to wake up David. Reading the notes, I took from the dream

God revealed to me was helpful to my interpretation process. Plus, I was happy that I did not disturb my husband during the night, and maybe this was the secret key to not waking him most nights. I took more time throughout the day to write out the dream, asking the Holy Spirit for direction and understanding.

As I continued using the book Victoria suggested, the book referred to Bible passages, which helped me decipher my dreams and visions, intensely seeking what God was trying to teach me or tell me. I started to feel some comfort with the direction and clarity toward what the heavenly Father has been calling me to do for Him or where He wanted me to grow within myself.

> *For to one is given through the Spirit the utterance of wisdom, and to another the utterance of knowledge according to the same Spirit, to another faith be the same Spirit, to another gifts of healing by one Spirit, to another the working of miracles, to another prophecy, to another the ability to distinguish between spirits, to another various kinds of tongues, to another the interpretation of tongues. All these are empowered by one and the same Spirit, who apportions to each one individually as he wills. (1 Corinthians 12:8–11 ESV)*

When I arrived at the church the following Sunday, I realized how the church had really changed for me in a year. Instead of the music pounding through my body, I found myself feeling centered with the Lord, singing His praises loudly like I did as a little girl. Being able to rejoice fully, arms raised, my spirit was soaring, longing to hear what the pastor was going to teach me from the Bible so I could receive the message God intended for me.

The pastor on this Sunday went on to suggest reading the entire Bible. I did not think much of it, but then he recommended it the following Sunday also. I questioned if this was even a possibility, not sure I would not be able to understand Scripture. I thought about how Julia mentioned the others prophesying in the Bible. When we got home, I brought this to Julia's attention, and she suggested getting a study Bible. My dreams still confused me, and I was eager to figure them out. No one I have met has ever really seemed to get this aspect of me. Still missing the mark that God was pointing out to me, I once again dismissed the thought of reading the Bible.

When the following Sunday came around, the pastor brought it up for the third time. This time around, he suggested reading the complete Bible in a year, and I thought this was an interesting concept. I could either read the Bible in a year and improve my understanding or not read it and still be in the same place. It left me wondering if I would have a better understanding of God's true direction for me and my calling.

Starting at the beginning of the Bible with the Old Testament, I found out it was more interesting than I thought it would be. There were battles and betrayal, kings who were influenced by the wrong people, brothers who played against their brothers, seductions and love stories, and others who did not want to listen to guidance and run away to find themselves lost. Yet this was a lot to take in. The Scripture was hard to understand at parts and made me question why God would do certain things in response to some situations.

I have been attempting to read the Bible now for many months and am only a little over halfway through the Old Testament. Then I start seeing things differently, and God is moving through people that I would have never thought He would use. I am starting to see the correlation where He chooses to use me even though He does not have to. He makes me worthy. I never really thought of it this way as I went about my day-to-day life, doing my day-to-day things, not considering if God would be thinking I was worthy or not. Now my thought processes are changing, and as I continue to plug along reading the Bible, I discover that Jesus has these plans for me. I thought I had an understanding of these stories as I heard them growing up: born from a virgin mother, did all these powerful healings, died on a cross, and rose from the dead on the third day. I am looking at this from a new perspective now of how different each of the apostles who came into play were. Jesus's journey, being a simple man, but fruitful of the soul and showing others how to live life where they do not carry shame and guilt. Contemplating what Jesus was showing me, He wanted me to receive His forgiveness and grace when I surrender all of me to Him, even the parts I had been embarrassed to show Him, understanding more fully His ascension into heaven to sit at the right hand of the

Father. I am learning that there are so many more intimate details I missed because I never took the time to read the Bible. It is changing my viewpoint over my days as I continue to forge ahead. For the first time, I am looking at life without judgment because Jesus is telling me that I am not the one who has to hold the weight of worry on my shoulders. God will take care of this. He *is* taking care of this, which is a physical relief inside me. As I continued reading the Scripture and learning more about others in the Bible who have prophetic dreams, the Lord opened my eyes to make me see this whole time my dreams were valid. I have always felt like I am crazy, but I am not crazy. There are other people that are written about in the ordained Word of God who is sent dreams from the heavenly realm. The only word I can think of to describe how I am feeling is *freedom*. Chains that have held me down for years have fallen off, and it was out of fear, not understanding, that I was responding to these dreams. Immediately I know they are beautiful messages from the Spirit and the gift of prophecy.

I am starting to see things with clarity, and I no longer have the element of fear blocking my viewpoint. Jesus wanted to show God's love to all the world, and He's using me in this way by teaching me about the Holy Spirit. He walks with me and guides me now... What a game changer. Jesus was showing me how to change every aspect of my life for the better despite my faults.

I noticed while reading the Bible that Jesus would go off alone to meditate. I have heard others at church talk about how creating space to hear from the Lord has helped them grow closer to understanding the Holy Spirit's direction and presence. God sent many in the Bible knowledge about interrupting their dreams through meditation, and I needed this next step. I need to comprehend my dreams to know the direction He is guiding me in. First, I had to figure out what that means and how to meditate.

I sank into the seat cushion on my back porch, lying my feet on the footstool, as the sun warmed my face. I closed my eyes and felt the light breeze across my body. I heard the wind rustling the leaves. There was a bird off in the distance chirping. I took a deep breath, and I concentrated on the sound of the chirp. Trying to stop thinking of everything that still needed to be done in my day, I began to feel my body relaxing. I took another deep breath and smelled the sweetness in the air, almost as if I was smelling the warmth of the sun. Starting to hum a song from the church in my head, every muscle was fully relaxed. It was like I could feel His presence around me, calming me, and inviting me into His presence. Opening my heart, my soul, and my mind to Him, I am inviting the Holy Spirit in. Peace over me, true peace, washes over me. Through meditation, I have discovered that I am creating room for the Holy Spirit to speak to me. I trust in Him.

Climbing under my cozy feather-down comforter for the night, my head relaxed into the pillow. I was trying mightily to shut my mind down from the day's activities. Before I fell asleep, I wanted to meditate.

Eyes closed, relaxed, *but do not fall asleep*. "Do not fall asleep," I was telling myself. I prayed to the Holy Spirit internally, *Please guide me and show me what You need me to learn during my sleep tonight through Your dreams and visions.*

While lying there relaxed, I found myself longing to be close to Him and to carry out His ways. I prayed that He would communicate with me so I could grow closer to Him. At the same time thinking about how it had been such a struggle for me to have others understand me, but yet a big part of me started not to care what others think of me anymore. The growing relationship I have with the heavenly Father is so amazing and fulfilling that nothing of this world that I have ever experienced has even come close.

*Trust in the Lord with all your heart, And lean
not on your own understanding; In all your ways
acknowledge Him, And He shall direct your paths.*
—Proverbs 3:5–6 NKJV

CHAPTER 11

Warning

The Father has shown me remarkable things, and attempting to distinguish what He is telling me through the language of dreams has been a huge learning process. Leaning mostly on the people who I feel know the Lord, my best friend, Alyson, has been wonderfully moved by the Spirit in ways that are unexplainable.

The sun was not even on the horizon yet, and as I held the cell phone in my hand, anxiously listening to it ringing, I hoped Alyson was awake enough to hear her cell and pick it up. Standing with a hot cup of coffee, looking out the sliding glass doors that lead out onto my patio, I was still able to see stars and a sliver of the moon's glow in the early morning sky. Hearing her voice say hi, I let out a sigh of relief. I haven't been able to sleep since the Lord shook me awake during the night with another vivid and intense dream. I can feel it in the depths of my bones... He is telling me something else is coming, just like the other two dreams about the wolves:

It was the present day, and I was walking west down the street I currently live on. The rays of sunshine brilliantly played across my face in the warm setting sun. I was inspecting the patches of violet and blue that stretched out across the sky to show the orange background well, breathing in the aroma of the hot air on a late summer evening. Gazing across the street, I suddenly became conscious of something on someone's garage door. It was a shadow. Stopping and pondering what this shadow was on their garage door for a moment, I seemed to know what it was, but my mind could not wrap my head around this object. The shadow on the garage door continued to grow. I started to cross the street at this point to look at the shadow closer, and that was when it hit me that the shadow was a tornado. It was rotating and twisting violently. I had just finished crossing over the street when I came to this conclusion. I looked over my right shoulder and up into the sky where the once beautiful sun was setting, now the sky was swirling with gray clouds, clouds that were dangerously dark, and it was coming without hesitation. Running out into the street, I started yelling at the cars and stretching my arms out in front of them.

I am screaming, "YOU ARE HEADING TOWARD A TORNADO! STOP, TURN AROUND, STOP, TORNADO!"

Screaming, my husband woke me up. He was telling me that it had been a while since he has had to wake me from a dream. I was very apologetic, but David was kind in nature and wrapped his arms around me. I continued to tell him about the dream, but he just told me it would all be okay and went back to sleep. Once again, troubled about what this could mean, and I knew I was done sleeping for the night. I tiptoed out of the room and went downstairs to make a pot of coffee, and I decided to write out the dream.

Talking to Alyson at this ungodly hour in the morning, we were discussing this very vivid dream. She brought up the thought and wondered if this was not another sign of the coronavirus coming back and maybe affecting us differently. Through these dreams, I am wishing I could understand God's messages for me so I could help His people in whatever way He intends. Heading off to work, entering the salon, I saw Julie, the other stylist I work with, who has walked this road graciously with me this whole time. Telling her what happened last night, she let me know she shared our concerns. We were both hoping God was telling me something different and not more about COVID-19, but it did not sound good either way. Months after this alarming dream going into fall and Christmas now in sight, the coronavirus has come back with vengeance. Just today—December 3, 2020—the state I live in Ohio reported 8,921 new cases, four-hundred more hospitalizations, and eighty-two deaths. God's dream warning me about the tornado coming appeared to be conclusive. The Holy Spirit has been intentional about honoring me with the gift of prophecy to help others and pray with them. I feel blessed that He chooses to use me.

*You did not choose me, but I chose you and appointed
you that you should go and bear fruit and that
your fruit should abide, so that whatever you ask
the Father in my name, he may give it to you.*
　　　　　　　　　　　　　　　—John 15:16 ESV

CHAPTER 12

God Speaks

Faith for me is like this: It stretches my limits, my boundaries, and my expectations. It makes me see things I never saw where there before. It prepares me to travel into situations I was never planning on walking into, and it takes me to places I never would have been able to find on my own. Faith is stretching my arms so far out in front of me that they hurt from the pulling of the way the heavenly Father is leading me to go.

Even though I am not seeing the way at this time, He keeps saying to me, *Just come, and you will see, I have this for you.*

Writing is not even close to being one of my strong points. Speaking correctly or even using proper grammar has not been an easy task for me. I am not sure if it was from the encephalitis and meningitis that there's an effect on my association with words, but I know that the Lord has seen greater things in me and is planting new seeds in my capacity. *That is faith coming in.* When I cannot even see a way, the Mighty Father is already moving mountains in my life behind the scenes. I limit my capabilities, but the Father is limitless.

Faith comes from trust, and even though I cannot see my next step, I know it will look different from what I think it is going to look like. I approach different situations, thinking it is going to look one way, but He has a much grander plan. He walks before me and beside me. He has seen the beginning and the end, and He will never let me fall. This is what I keep telling myself for faith has a way of being hard to hear even when it is coming from the heavenly Father. Now, taking my hands off my ears and opening my eyes, I was overwhelmed with awe as He came to me at night:

His voice was beyond brilliant. It sounded like a thousand voices all in one, and my lungs were seizing for it was breathtaking, almost not being able to speak in response to the sound.

He is calling on me? My thoughts were spinning.

The Lord went on to say, *I want you to write my book.*

Stunned. I said, "Yes, I am your humble servant. I will do whatever You want me to do."

I said these words with intention in my heart which was pounding intensely. My hands were shaking.

The beautiful Father went on to say to me, *Name the book, All the Glory Goes to God.* And He gently put me back to sleep.

Immediately upon awakening, I remembered the Lord's invitation. My heart started racing along with my mind feeling anticipation, astonishment, and being amazed that the heavenly Lord visited me during the night.

I thought, *I love You, Lord with all my heart, but I cannot do this! I can't even put a normal English sentence together, yet alone write a book. How am I going to write Your book and name it All the Glory Goes to God? What would I say?*

It was like He was right there, hearing my thoughts because it was in that moment that the Holy Spirit then pressed on my heart and reminded me of the prophetic dream He gave me a year earlier. The dream that was the remembrance of the space where God sustained my existence while I slept during my coma as a little girl and when He communicated to me that He exquisitely loves me and His creation to the core of our beings. He then continued to lean on my heart for I needed to write this book for other moms, dads, or loved ones. I could feel Him letting my spirit know that there are hearts suffering over someone who is sick or burdened or unreachable in their worlds who needed to hear what He was teaching me. The heavenly Father wants them to know that He has their loved ones safe and wrapped up in His arms, protecting them.

Moses walked in faith. He was called by faith. The Father chose to speak to Moses, and he listened. It was written in Exodus 4:10–12 (NLT):

> But Moses pleaded with the Lord,
> "O Lord, I'm not very good with words.
> I never have been, and I'm not now, even

though you have spoken to me. I get tongue-tied, and my words get tangled." Then the Lord asked Moses, "Who makes a person's mouth? Who decides whether people speak or do not speak, hear or do not hear, see or do not see? Is it not I, the Lord? Now go! I will be with you as you speak, and I will instruct you in what to say."

In this little way, I lean on how the Lord responded to Moses when his faith was lacking in confidence and trust that the Lord will be with me as I write.

Who could I say that the Lord just woke me up in the middle of the night and told me to write His book? The Lord continued to place a name in my head. I knew this person in my life would be kind and, in his goodness, help me to progress on the calling of God. If I were to be obedient to the dream, this individual would be a light in my darkness by helping me clean up my writing and teach me a handful of editing skills. I am good friends with his wife, Sue, and she will only think I am half crazy with my proposal. I had the feeling you get when you can feel your spirit in alignment with the path that the Lord has written for you, and you are filled with excitement, fear, and wonder. It was overwhelming but in a good way.

Jumping out of bed, I rushed downstairs and called the couple. There was no hesitation in her or her husband's, Dennis, voice to help me. I was pleasantly surprised, but I also found myself aware that I should not be for when

God says He is going to do it, I believe it will be done. I decided to tell no one at first besides the one who the Lord put on my heart to help me with this process. I had not the slightest idea where to start, but I created some time before dinner later that day.

I sat down with a notepad in hand, and I asked, "Holy Spirit, please show me what You would like me to write."

And then it flowed out of me, flowing from pen to paper, creating the pages that you have been reading now. Ideas that I knew had to be coming from the Lord for my mind is only half creative on its own, and hearing the Holy Spirit guide me was exactly what I was praying for. This is not my book. God asked me to write His book, so I am writing to testify to others of His endless and unconditional love which He wants all of us to receive.

Weeks passed, and I really wanted to share with Julia about the dream God sent me, asking me to write His book. In telling her, I went on to disclose that I did not know why, but I felt I couldn't tell anyone that I was writing this book.

She calmly listened and went on to explain, "Mom, you are listening to the Holy Spirit, and He might want you to protect this book for now. You will be subjected to other people's influences if you openly discuss what the Holy Spirit is in the process of pruning."

Wow, that makes so much sense. How did this young lady get so smart? I took that to heart and left it only with those three individuals. Months passed, and I knew I needed to let my husband in on it. I figured he was starting to wonder why I was on the computer to this extent because I never spent time on the computer.

Finding David upstairs in our bedroom, I asked him if he had a quick second.

He said, "Sure."

I went on to tell him the whole story and how God asked me to write this book for Him, and I could feel my body tensing because I was nervous about his reaction. He had heard me wakened from crazy dreams, and he had watched me become a stronger woman through my relationship with the Lord. But also I too know how the thought of me being ordained by God must sound. I have been married to this man for fourteen years, and I can read his facial reactions unmistakably well. Let me tell you, this man did not even flinch. He was instantly supportive and thought it was great that I was trying to write. *Did not see that one coming.* Here I was so nervous, not sure what his reaction was going to be, and he showed up loving and supportive. He still can surprise me by the way he shows me love and kindness.

God was just moving mountains around me! Or people were just keeping their thoughts to themselves. Either way, I was glad that I was truly writing the book God called me to! I was genuinely appreciative that God suggested Dennis and Sue. He always knows best. When I would send them a chapter, they would gently guide me toward where I needed improvement—never belittling me or making me feel less than but instead sending constructive criticism my way.

I continued to write every chance I got, astonished by how often the Lord continues to send me dreams to guide me through the process. He sent me another significant dream this week:

I bit my tongue so hard. My hand was coming up to my mouth when I heard the Father say in a strong voice, *Speak*!

Waking up stunned, thinking I was going to be in great pain, I reached for my tongue, comforted by the fact that I did not bite it at all. I was awestruck upon hearing the Father's voice. It was strong and forceful. The definition of *powerful.*

Lying in bed, processing, God started showing me visions. The first vision was a glass of water that was full, and it fell over with water spilling out. Second, there was an open book showing words that I could not depict, not sure if it was the Bible or just a thick book. Third, the word *h u s b a n d* was printed out.

I was moved by the beauty the Lord revealed to me in these moments of stillness, wanting to discern where He was guiding me. As soon as I got up, I turned to my friend who had written books on her own prophecies and curious to get her input on what the heavenly Father might be saying.

Paige's response was, "I believe God is calling us to speak boldly about who He is and what we can do through Him in a world that is trying very hard to suppress the truth. Remember that the Lord is your Bridegroom—the One who provides Living Water to all who come to drink."

He is my Bridegroom, stopping to meditate on this dream along with her input, the one thing I kept receiving from the Holy Spirit was that I continued too not be bold enough to speak up for my heavenly Father. It is time for me to share these amazing gifts He has given me. He is not saying I should profess it to strangers while standing on a street corner, but rather, God is telling me to share His love and grace with people in my life that I have neglected to do so. He showed me the exquisite knowledge of unconditional love, which I experienced during the coma. Now, the Father is continuing to watch as I break free of my chains, leave my comfort zone, and grow closer to Him. He is telling me that it is my job to acknowledge what He has given me and tell others about it. The Lord is telling me to SPEAK about Him. A few days later, the heavenly Father gave me another glorious dream:

I was the yolk in the middle of an egg, thinking about moving into the white part (or the albumen); however, I was scared. I decided to move into the white part of the egg just a little bit, but then I backed up inside the yellow yoke. All of a sudden, I saw the shell crack, and I could hear this beautiful voice. It was the Father singing a poem over me.

The clock read 2:06 a.m. As joy-filled tears escaped my eyes, I reached for my notepad and started scribbling down as fast as I could to remember the words of the poem that the heavenly Father was singing over me. But I could only capture these few words before they slipped from my memory.

> When the shell cracked, the child hid,
> but the Father sang, *Come out for you will
> be one of my own for the beauty is what is
> inside*… And the Father continued to sing.
> His voice was so marvelously beautiful.

I was so excited, elated, for I was able to hear the Lord singing over me. The most elegant singing I have ever heard. Graceful and loving. I was lost in amazement over His voice singing over *me*. Even if I was a yellow yoke in the dream and not in my human form, I looked forward to how my friend from church, Victoria, will interrupt God's message to me. I sent her a text message, and she responded by explaining in a text her understanding of what He was telling me:

> The egg dream is that God loves you. You are covered and protected. You are growing, and He is getting ready to bring you out.

How meaningful that Victoria explained how God has covered and protected me, that He knows me better than anyone else, knowing it is safe to bring me out of the secret place inside of myself. The heavenly Father is proclaiming that it's my time to walk in alignment with the calling that has been meant for me all along.

Looking at my life, I realize there are pivotal moments when I could have made a change. There have been moments when something deep within me has called me, and I have had the option to follow that intuition. But instead, I have traveled in the opposite direction. In my heart, deep in my heart, that one true voice is the Lord, and He is calling me. He is reaching deep enough to rescue me, and He is rescuing me from myself. He is wanting me to go down a new path with Him, one that is a wonderful path, a true path that is different from anything I have ever walked before. It is new, it is change, and it scares me. I cannot see where it is leading, so I have turned away from it time and time again when I have reached that fork in the road. In that pivotal moment, I have always decided to go down the path that I am familiar with, instead of going down the path that my heart keeps longing to go down. Fear has held me in place.

Reach. I need to reach deep into my soul to make the commitment to taking this new path. It should not scare me for I think about my inner child who has walked this path before. She has played there, loved there, and laughed there. I fear it now because as an adult I have been hurt, doubt sets in. But somewhere deep, deep inside of me, I know this is not of God. This is of humans speaking through criticism and social media that has allowed me to believe the lies of this world. God will never hurt me. The Lord might show me things on this path that I do not want to confront, but I am finally ready to go on the journey. I have been hesitant to follow and to listen to the voice that calls, but those yearns in my soul to go are more powerful than the spirit of fear.

I take a step forward on the path. He is having me confront the issues I have rooted deep within myself. As I make more footprints on this path, I am realizing each step I take is leading me to true freedom, and He has not left me, rather He has been right beside me as I have been walking. Through my obedience, He has met me where I am by showing me so much love and freedom, just like in the dream which brought me unconditional love. I thought

I might not be able to attain it in this world, but the Father is showing me daily more and more of His beauty, grace, and abundant life which He offers as I travel this path with Him.

> *For I am the Lord your God who takes*
> *hold of your right hand and says to you, Do*
> *not fear; I will help you. (Isaiah 41:13 NIV)*

I thought if God knew my viewpoints on certain matters that might or might not coincide with the Bible, then He would not love me. Suppose God knew some of the crazy things I did in my youth, He would not love me. Or I have gotten divorced, well, you know what that means… When I had the experience where God's eminent love was given to all of us during the time I spent in a coma, He showed me there is nothing that can separate me from His abundance of love. However, even after that incredible life-changing experience, I still had trouble believing God could love me. Like I said in the beginning, I did not even think my own human father was very fond of me. This unfortunately was how I felt. My viewpoint of a father was very obscured. Years before my father's passing, I came to peace and acceptance within myself over my earthly dad, realizing he did the best he could with what he was brought up knowing.

Then feeling God's love engulfs me, His loving embrace and not just for me but for every child, no matter the race, sex, or ethnic heritage. I could not help but know now that God is love, an abiding love that cannot and will not separate unless I choose to not let Him in. I did not for a long time. I still do not have to. I have free will. And I am good at making a mess of things in my life. I have suffered from depression and anxiety. When I walk with the Holy Spirit and I start to feel anxious or depressed, He is there guiding, loving, and showing me a way through my troubles. Many times as my children were growing up, I would tell them God loves them, and I think on some surface level I thought God loved me. But deep, deep down inside me, I just did not believe or really trust it. As a little girl, I knew somehow that God loved me. I felt His love singing over me. This was a long time ago. By revealing where He sustained me as a child, I felt the magnitude of love again, His grace, and mercy.

And I am convinced that nothing can ever separate us from God's love. Neither death nor life, neither angels nor demons, neither our fears for today nor our worries about tomorrow— not even the powers of hell can separate us from God's love. No power in the sky above or in the earth below—indeed, nothing in all creation will ever be able to separate us from the love of God that is revealed in Christ Jesus our Lord.
—Romans 8:38–39 NLT

CHAPTER 13

Obedience

Throughout my life, my earthly father always referred to me as being stupid. He would not hesitate to state that it was not a good idea for me to go to college, but I always had a love for art and excelled in it. By the time I was ready to graduate high school, I knew I needed a plan, and college was "not an option." I decided to go to a beauty academy and study how to become a professional beautician. Being a stylist opened the opportunity to allow me to continue to use my artistic skills, so when I felt the Lord pressing on my heart to leave this career field after thirty-plus years in the industry, I was positive I was not hearing Him correctly.

So I stepped back and thought about this past year, *Did He leave me signs?*

Walking in the door at work, I looked over at Julie and said, "I had another dream last night that God sent me about the salon. It was the third one this month."

I went on to tell her what the dream was about; however, this time, I told her that I felt a pull to leave the salon, "The Holy Spirit has been pressing on my heart for some time now to leave."

As I continued to explain, I was also thinking, *But where would I go?*

I have no other skill. I have only known this practice my entire life.

At one point, I looked around this little salon where I have worked for such a long time and felt very melancholy. I have experienced so much of my life in these walls…my pregnancies, going through my divorce, meeting the love of my life, and getting remarried. It truly is my second home. My boss was more of a friend than a boss, and it troubled me to even think of telling her I could be leaving. Going and sitting down in the break room, taking a drink of water, I could feel the Holy Spirit deep within me, trying to tell me it was time to leave. Trying to push those thoughts down because there seemed to be a more important matter at hand, everyone was talking about this thing called the coronavirus and how it had just turned up in the United States.

COVID-19 was hitting the United States, and the government had closed the beauty shop for two months. During this time, I realized God might be onto something for I really had needed a break from work. Returning in May, I had this sinking feeling that I was not supposed to be back at the salon. Although, I decided to set these feelings aside because some of my customers had become like family to me, and it would be hard to walk away.

The Lord had given me signs. I tried to put blinders on my eyes, but the Lord was being persistent, presenting me with another questioning dream as I slept:

I stood behind my customer at the beauty shop, cutting her hair when I abruptly stopped and set my scissors down on the counter. I turned, started heading to the door, and walked right out of the salon. Strolling down the little path outside, I looked up on the horizon as the sun was setting in the evening sky. The dazzling colors played off each other, and an open field in front of me glowed green with dandelions and clovers covering it. I found my soul longing to go out into the field, but I decided to then turn back instead, down the little path. Upon opening the door to the salon, it was totally empty. Nothing was left. The only thing there was the cement floor.

I instantly awakened in the middle of the night, almost like a snap of my fingers, lying there thinking about this dream. I decided to get up and go downstairs. Because once again, I was done sleeping for the night. My head was pondering all of what the Holy Spirit was asking of me. *Am I hearing Him correctly?* One and a half years ago, my husband started his own business, and it had not taken off yet which means that for the time being, I was the only one bringing money into the household.

I said to the Lord, "God, how about this? If You want me to quit my job, could you please let David's purchase order have an official confirmation, and then I will know that You are guiding me to leave?"

Yes, that was it. I was going to ask for a sign, one which will reassure me that I should leave my job. Thinking about this, I know others asked for signs in the Bible, so this makes sense, yes?

Christmas came and went. It was a new year, and God was still diligent and continued to give me dreams where I felt He was asking me to leave my job in faith and in obedience. I was scared. What would we possibly do to have money coming in throughout this season of our lives? Nothing had changed on the projection of my husband's company. I was proud of him, and we were confident. But we were still waiting for the order to be approved.

Easter was here and gone. Holy cow, a whole year just went by. I was still at the salon and not listening to His instructions. The Holy Spirit was leaning heavily on my heart to go on to the next chapter and to have faith, but the whole thing just sounded ridiculous to me...to leave my job while my husband's business still hadn't been set in stone and things were so financially tight? It seemed almost as if it would be selfish.

The sweetness of June has arrived with the sun already high in the sky on this early Sunday morning. My feet hit the pavement. I slammed the car door behind me and rushed in the door of the sanctuary to church. It was so dark I was having trouble finding my daughter, but when I finally spot her, I realized that she was sitting way up in the front, almost in the middle of the aisle. And I let out a sigh. I was one of those people who like to sit off to the side and kind of hide.

But whatever, I was thinking in my head, excusing myself as I climb over others to sit next to her, relieved to have made it before service started.]

That day, the church had a guest speaker, and as she talked, something was troubling my brain. I felt uncomfortable, but I could not put my finger on what I was internally agonizing over. Her sermon was about whether we were going to be obedient to where God was calling us or if we would be disobedient. As I continued listening, she was getting to the end of her lesson, and the Holy Spirit called me right out. I could hear His voice speaking directly to me, clearly saying two words: One was the name of the salon that I worked, and the other was my husband's project that he had been waiting on the purchase order for, which was also what I wanted my next step to be—the next place where I really would like to work. I knew exactly what the Holy Spirit was saying in just two words. No more was needed to understand the message from the Holy Spirit. Tears flooded my face, *right then*. Sitting up front, in the middle of the aisle, surrounded by others, during service, I was crying.

God was asking, *Are you going to be obedient?*

All the way home in the car, I talked to the Holy Spirit in my head, asking Him, *How long should I give work notice? I have worked at just this salon for the last twenty-nine years. I feel bad just leaving.*

I kept hearing the Holy Spirit say, *Seven weeks*

I said to Him, *If that is right and I am hearing You correctly, then please show me signs. I don't mean to doubt, but please, show me your confirmation.*

Seven started showing up everywhere I looked as I drove home. I thought that could be coincidental; however, when I checked the calendar on my phone, it was August 1.

For me, it just seemed to make sense because it was a solid date to tell my boss when I would be leaving my job, and I would be providing her with plenty of notice.

Then I started to feel a little anxious, and my thoughts had me spiraling. I began wondering how my husband would react with no income coming into the family for this really seemed like a big leap of faith on his part. I invited the Holy Spirit to be with me when I walked in the door and saw David in the kitchen, making lunch.

He asked if I was hungry, and I told him, "No, not really."

But it was mostly because I was a bundle of nerves. David went around the counter and sat at the table. The Sunday afternoon sun was streaming in the sliding screen doors, and I could see two squirrels chasing each other around in the yard. Walking over and sitting down at the table with his sandwhich, I took a deep breath and held it in. With a heavy exhale, I lung into the story while he ate his sandwich. I was not leaving out a detail of what I experienced at church and the input I felt I received from the Holy Spirit as I drove home. He let me speak, which was good because my stomach was in knots, and I felt like vomiting on him. But once I caught my breath, he responded with immaculate love. He was so supportive, never stopping for a second of indecision, and told me that we would make it work. Now do not get me wrong. My husband is a sweetheart, but I was starting to question my own sanity because this decision seemed honestly scary.

Several weeks passed. Church just ended, and a young woman came up to me.

She introduced herself and said, "This is going to sound weird, but the Holy Spirit the last couple of weeks has been telling me I need to talk to you. But I do not know why?"

I chuckled. "Not sure this is what it is about but," I continued as I went on to tell her I just gave my job of twenty-nine years my notice a couple of weeks back and how I had no other job lined up. She looked at me and smiled, saying to me that now she knew why the Holy Spirit wanted her to talk to me.

I said, "Really?"

She explained that two years ago, she also took this leap of faith and had no other job awaiting her. Once deciding upon leaving her job, she pledged to be obedient to the Holy Spirit—and she didn't just get a new job. She got an amazing position earning a higher salary.

Hmm…that sounds great, I thought.

She told me about a book she received from a friend that really helped her during this time. It was about the book of Hebrews, centering its focus on chapters 11 and 12. She said she would bring it next week, and I thanked her. We departed, but all I kept thinking about was our conversation.

Is this why I have been stuck for so long? Am I not listening? I am not being obedient?

The following Sunday, after receiving the book about a couple of chapters out of Hebrews, I brought the book out to my screened porch and curled up on the couch. Feeling the warm summer breeze, I sat and read. With this book being a study guide, I never looked at Hebrews from the perspective now offered to me. I found out that Abel, Enoch, Noah, Abraham, Sarah, Moses, and many more written about in the Bible had stepped out in faith on their journey with God. I had not ever really looked at it from this point of view. They just listened to God's call and went. Some did not even get to see His promises come into fruition, but it did not matter for they had true faith in His calling.

> *Faith is being sure of what we hope for.*
> *It is being sure of what we do not see.*
> *We have faith. So we understand that everything was made when God commanded it. That's why we believe that what we see was not made out of what could be seen. (Hebrews 11:1–3 NIV)*

Finishing the study guide book, I was amazed by the insight the author had about Hebrews chapters 11 and 12. I knew that because I was being obedient. The Holy Spirit was going to bless me with the job that He had intentionally created the space for me in. If it was not the one working with my husband, I had the faith that some other amazing job would come to fill its place.

I had one more week left to work at the salon.

Panic was starting to race through my mind, and I was thinking, *What are we going to do for income?*

I asked my boss at the salon if I could stay on for a few more weeks but only for a couple days each week.

I am still being obedient, right? My gut was kicking me.

Still no news on a new job and I knew I needed to leap if I was going to trust in the Lord with all my heart.

He showed me in a dream last night that I was still not being obedient. I was frustrated with being stuck in the same place, ready for the Holy Spirit to show me what I needed to work through, whatever it was, so I could grow closer to Him.

In one week, I had three comparable dreams, each of different people I had known who died throughout my life. In each dream, we were at the beauty shop. They seemed to have a clear message, and they were all telling me that I needed to be obedient and leave the salon.

Walking back and forth in my front yard, the chilly wind whipped through me as I tried to use the leaf blower to get the leaves to the curb. Thanksgiving is next week, and as the leaves kept blowing back in my face, all I could think about was the fact that I really thought once I left my job and was obedient, You, God would give me an amazing job immediately. I was undoubtedly confident that I had figured out this obedience thing, and now I felt really broken down. Not working was making me feel very exposed and vulnerable. I set the blower down and sat in the cold grass.

I was second-guessing everything in my mind… *Did I hear Him right? Did He really tell me to leave my job? Was that what the dreams were telling me? What am I going to do? What are You telling me, Lord? My husband's order has not come through yet so I cannot go work for him.*

In the past weeks, I talked to others at church about my situation, and they kept saying, "Be obedient."

I get it, *but*. There always is a but. I was now finding myself on my knees in the cold grass as a very weepy version of myself.

Worn out from worry and trying to understand God's directions, I asked Him for guidance before I climbed into bed for the night. Sleeping, He showered me with blessings:

There was a little girl, maybe around five years old, with darkness all around her. She did not seem to be afraid. She stood to the left of the scene that I was watching, and to my right, there was the Father about ten feet away. He got down on one knee and stretched both His arms out to her. She ran to Him, and He immersed her in His arms. The love I felt was overflowing.

Upon awakening in the middle of the night, my body was overwhelmed with a feeling of love. I knew right in this instant He was telling me that He had me and that He wanted to give me everything if I let Him. In this moment, He revealed to me that I was choosing to block Him, even in the ways that He wanted to give me His riches. *The heavenly Lord wants to give me His riches*! This surprised me for I wasn't just blocking myself from His love, but I was blocking myself from all His abundance in this world. There had been so much more He had been wanting to give me, and I was withholding it from myself.

The following night, the heavenly Father sent me another dream:

The late warm summer evening sun was casting shadows, letting me know it was getting ready to set. I stood in the front yard of the house I grew up in, close to the front steps that lead out to the driveway. I noticed three of my sisters were a few feet away from me, shifting my eyes at once to observe my parents having a yard sale. Mostly what was left were three porch swings, and I told my sisters how I would really love to have one of those for my house. The porch swing I was eyeing was suspended in the air, and rays of sunlight were reflecting iridescent colors. The swing was a brilliant pale blue, composed of white traces around the outside. My one sister, Rose, encouraged me to go and tell Dad, but I grew hesitant because I feared He would say no. That was when all three of my sisters continued to persuade me to go, yet I still resisted even though something inside of me longed to go. My fear held me back from asking, and I chose not to move.

Upon awakening, I experienced the darkness all around me, a glow reflected from the clock on the night-stand. I reached down and grabbed the comforter and pulled it up over me, hearing the gentle rain against the window frame, pondering the message of what the Lord could be telling me. When the Holy Spirit helped me recognize that this pertained to the dream the night before also, I had the understanding that my sisters in this dream were angels. They were trying to tell me that the heavenly Father wanted me to go and have a seat in His chair and that there was nothing He will withhold from me. It was *I* who withheld myself from His riches because He was welcoming and wanted to give it all to me. I then started to pray with the Holy Spirit, specifically seeking out His help to guide me to be open to His gifts and to be truly open to let them flow in and through my life. I sat in His stillness and was meditating on His abundance.

When I fell back asleep, the Lord continued to show me this night His prosperity of what He has been holding for me. As the night wore on, I awakened with a number in my mind's eye. I rolled over and wrote it down on the notepad next to my bed. I began thinking about how God did not show me numbers very often in my dreams, but my mind and body were just too tired to mull this over for too long. And I drifted back to sleep.

Today I was up and going, refreshed and energized by the graciousness of the Father wanting to give me all His riches. In all His love, I knew that I no longer must block myself from allowing this in my life. Suddenly, I heard my husband calling out to me from his office. I ran up the stairs and around the corner for this was not like him. My mind was questioning what all this fuss was over as I swung open his office door to see that he had the biggest smile on his face.

David exclaimed, "I received the purchase order!"

He continued to tell me the details, and in translation, he mentioned the number of how many had been ordered. A flash instantly went through my mind of the number I wrote down on the notepad during the night, but the only difference was the digits were in reverse. I had not been thinking about what I wrote when I awoke in the morning, but once he received the purchase order, I knew God was reminding me of the dream last night. God was sending confirmation of how He had me and of all that the Lord wanted to give me if I was open to Him and His ways. The second David received the purchase order, I was given the opportunity to start a new career! Obedience from me aligns with abundance from the heavenly Father. God wants to give me abundance…abundance of love that overflows and fills the atmosphere in every area of my life, and I have been blocking myself from receiving it. I needed to seek Him first.

The Lord will open the heavens, the storehouse of his bounty, to send rain on your land in season and to bless all the work of your hands. You will lend to many nations but will borrow from none.
—Deuteronomy 28:12 NIV

CHAPTER 14

Listening

My mother is settled in an assisted living community, luckily not too far from my home, and her disease has progressed slowly. The doctors call it a spectrum of dementia. She has her good days and her bad ones. Some days, she remembers me, and other days, she knows I am one of her children but not sure which one. I have long since gotten used to this and love what was once left of my mother.

Scrubbing the kitchen sink, the window above was open, and I could feel a light warm breeze coming in. The sun shone high in the afternoon sky and was streaming right through the window. Cheerfully singing off-key, as I scrubbed away, my fluffy white cockapoo puppy soared up the stairs because he was dissatisfied with my singing. I heard the side door open, and I turned to see Julia coming in. She was distressed and weeping uncontrollably. My mom's alarm instinctively went off.

"What is wrong?" I asked her.

When I rushed to her, she was stuttering her words, and I could not understand her because she was crying so hard.

"Slow down. What happened?"

Trying to breathe calmly, I was not sure what she was about to tell me.

Julia blurted out, "I just saw Grandma, and she did not remember who I was."

My whole body softened, yet I, too, could feel that ache in my heart right then. I encompassed her in my arms. There were no words to express what was happening to this once loving woman who adored her grandchildren. You could see it was tearing Julia apart. My heart was crumbling to see Julia in so much emotional pain for her relationship with her grandmother had always been divinely tight.

God does not leave me in these times. He never does. He is right there showing up and giving me the strength I need. My heart was full of questions for the Lord as I climbed under the covers and fell into a deep sleep.

My thoughts were puzzling me as I stood in the bedroom doorway of my girlfriend's, Melissa, house. There was colorful tissue and wrapping paper thrown all over the room, shocked by what I was looking at. If you knew me, you would know that any mess of any significance in my environment causes much confusion. I continued into the room. There were boxes to my left, and I went into the one box to take out its contents. It held a doll, and she was very fragile, made of tissue paper, and missing one black eye. I set her down on top of some of the boxes which were piled high off to the right of me, then I knelt on the floor to start wrapping gifts. Upon opening the boxes to put gifts in, I found they were stuffed with bunched-up wrapping paper. My girlfriend entered the room from a door across the way, and she was all excited because she bought me a present. She handed it to me, and I opened the gift immediately. She bought me an intricate jewelry box. I was delighted and set it beside myself on the floor. The whole time she had been in the room with me, she had been on the phone with her husband, Carl, but then she enthusiastically walked out of the room, continuing to talk with him. There was a bathroom connected to the bedroom behind me where Melissa just walked into while she continued to talk on the phone to her husband. They were an older couple, and his health had not been well. I decided to get up off the floor and follow her into the bathroom. Coming along the side of her where she was standing over by the bathroom sink, taking pills out of the medicine cabinet. Clearly overhearing her husband on the phone, he told her that she needed to watch what she was eating because he was concerned for her. I was pondering this thought because it was Carl, her husband, that had the main health concerns here.

My dream ended and flowed into a second dream:

My mom and I are at a restaurant staging the place for a party. The tables were already exquisitely decorated with glorious flower arrangements invading the middle of all the tables with brilliantly lit candles. The restaurant had wooden beams on the ceiling, and the party room was connected to the main restaurant, separated by a bar off to the right. I was busy putting silverware on the tables. As I finished up, I walked over to another table where more supplies were stacked up. Opening one of the boxes, I looked inside and saw dishes that were all individually wrapped up in brown paper. I took one out at a time because the dishes were all delicate and lovely, when I came across one that had a chip in it, I set it aside. Once I gathered all the dishes, I bunched the paper up and stuck it back into the box, grabbing the stack and carrying them to the table to begin placing them in their appropriate place settings. I stopped and watched my mom for a moment... It was nice to see her so happy. She was busy working away, getting everything ready for the party. I was almost done placing the last dish on the table when I surveyed the room and noticed one of my sisters entering the restaurant. She was followed by my other sisters, and they were bringing all kinds of wonderful casseroles in their hands. My one sister then approached me with her casserole in hand, and she stopped to look at me as if she was about to ask me a question.

I looked at her and said, "I brought the cake."

I woke up abruptly in the middle of the night, and I tried to figure out what the Lord was wanting to tell me in both these dreams. They certainly seemed unconnected. A running thought flashed through my mind. In Genesis 41:25, Joseph interpreted two of Pharaoh's dreams. King Pharaoh of Egypt could not figure out what his dreams meant, and Joseph asked God to explain them to him on the king's behalf. The interpretation of the dreams that Pharaoh was having both had the same meaning. God was telling Pharaoh what would happen soon: The seven good cows from the first dream and the seven good heads of grain from the second dream were seven good years of great abundance. The seven lean, ugly cows from the first dream and the seven worthless heads of grain scorched by the east wind from the second dream were seven years of famine. God was telling the King there would be seven years of hunger to follow the seven good years of feast. For Pharaoh to prepare, he would need to save some of their harvests for the seven bad years prophesied. Trying diligently to understand what the Holy Spirit was telling me through these two dreams He just sent me, thinking about the purpose of this Bible passage, I asked if the Holy Spirit would please send a divine interpretation.

Closing my eyes, relaxing into a calm, tranquil state in my field of vision, I saw a shadow of an angel. I felt wonder arise but tried to stay calm because I really wanted to know the answer. The angel first showed me the tissue paper doll with one eye missing.

I said to the angel in my mind, *No, no. This has to do with my girlfriend, not the paper doll!* In my justification, I saw the angel starting to vanish. Panic surged through me, and I proclaimed internally, *Please wait! Please wait, I am so sorry. Please show me what you are telling me!*

The angel slowly reappeared as a shadow off in the distance. I breathed a sigh of relief, filled with gratitude. The angel showed me again the tissue paper doll with the one black eye missing and then took me to the other dream, showing me the beautiful plate with the chip in it. I heard the words *life fragile*. The angel took me back to the first dream, showing me next to the bunched-up tissue paper in the box, and then compared it with the other dream of the brown paper and me bunching it up and putting it in the box. I heard the word *unravel.*

Lastly, the angel showed me Melissa talking to Carl on the phone in the bathroom and overhearing his concern for her diet. Then back to the other dream to show me my sisters bringing food and me saying, *I brought the cake.* I heard the angel say, *Misguided.*

Three words: life fragile, unravel, and misguided.

At once, the angel vanquished.

I lay there astonished and grateful for the guidance God sent through the holy presence of His angel. I would have never picked up on the eye-missing doll or the chipped dish with the bunched paper and misplaced concern. Life is fragile, and it is going by quickly. It made me think once again that I need to let others know how much the heavenly Father loves all of us unconditionally in all our incompleteness, allowing God to *unravel* the truth in me if I open myself up to seeing what is buried deep within myself to break the chains that keep me bound from experiencing true freedom. The thought of unraveling those things that are so deeply hidden is what scares me for I may not even be aware of the deep-seated roots because they are under so many layers. Today, I need to let God help me confront and restore all parts of my heart to have genuine healing. He is showing me the anxiety I have placed over conditions which I gave great importance to was misguided—spending so much of my day stressing over meaningless things, like will my kids attend the "right" college or what others will think of what college they attend or what car I drive or if my kitchen or my bathroom needs to be remodeled.

Misguided. I misguided myself, putting status on these things and feeling I am supposed to want them. The world is unraveling to me for the first time, and I am seeing it through a magnifying lens. Life is fragile, and as it unravels in front of me, I find the genuine joy God has for me comes from letting go of the misguidance I have been following all my life.

My dreams have been a vessel for me to get guidance from the Father who is moving behind the scenes in my life. Even when it comes to my own mother, I would never want to see her have to go down a road where she doesn't seem to recognize the world around her. Unraveling God's truths as I walk my days is sometimes not for me to understand but to simply accept and trust that He has a plan much greater than I can foresee. I can drive myself crazy with questions regarding why He would allow this to happen to her and why all these horrible things happen in the world, but... life fragile, unravel, and misguided. He showed me in the picturesque warehouse at five years old the riches of love He has for all of us, consuming every part of our being and loving us to the core of our beings. I know now that some things are so far beyond my comprehension. It is just not for me to know but to have faith that God has a refined plan. I will learn from whatever experiences I go through on my journey because it has been written by God. If I choose to trust and walk with Him, I will be much lighter. Freer. Life is more rewarding when I take the time to see Him everywhere in everything, walking with Him I have a newfound freedom.

May the God of hope fill you with all joy and peace as you trust in him, so that you may overflow with hope by the power of the Holy Spirit.
—Romans 15:13 NIV

CHAPTER 15

To Feed

God will prepare the food, but we must feed the people. My subconsciousness was still transparent as I awake to the heavenly Father speaking these words over me: *God will prepare the food, but we must feed the people.* Reflecting on this meaningful recollection, burying myself under the covers, I could hear the sharp winter winds howling outside my bedroom window. The snow sounded like ice pellets whipping against the side of the house forcefully. As I quieted my thoughts, the Holy Spirit pressed on my heart the Scripture where Jesus feeds five thousand: "And they said to Him, 'We have here only five loaves and two fish'" (Matthew 14:17 NKJV)). The Holy Spirit continued to explain to me the sentence the heavenly Father told me from this passage. What the apostles had thought insufficient amounts of food to feed five thousand people, Jesus had already foreseen the great miracle and provided it by looking to heaven and blessing the bread and fish, then multiplied the five loaves and two fish. When I feel like my talents, my time, and my contributions are insignificant, even though I cannot see the outcome, Jesus is multiplying them behind the scenes.

I have been caught in an illusion all my life, allowing myself to be pulled into worldly beliefs about the way I look and the way I should talk, think, and live. People have opinions on whether I am too fat, too thin, wearing the right clothes, or if my hair is the right shade, but it is all an illusion. God revealed to me that I am stuck in the illusion of what you think you really want or just can't live without or what others tell you that you must have, and I believed the lie.

He said, *Let me show you. You are a tree, with roots that run deep, and I will supply the water. I will be your stream. As your roots will drink and you absorb more of my Word through My living water, your tree will grow strong. You will form secure branches which will be able to hold great weight, and leaves will flourish out of them. As the roots continue to drink, you will feel the warmth of my sunlight upon your leaves, and then buds will form, producing exceptional fruit which will qualify you to feed my people. This is what I have planned for you all along...such great success. The splendor I have seen inside of you, to help others to achieve their growth by your nourishment that all comes from My nourishment, is because all the glory comes from Me, from the true Living Water.*

God will prepare the food, but we must feed the people.

As I had been stepping out of the illusion, I realized God was not telling me I was not supposed to not want things, He wanted to give me abundance. But I was looking at life from the wrong perspective. My soul I felt was dying from anxiety and depression because the piece I kept missing was the Lord, and not fulfilling my soul's purpose, which is honoring the talents the Lord gave me. As a child, I had been so close to the Lord for I honored who I was, a carefree child. Letting go and embracing exactly who I am as an adult, not what the world thinks I should be, but who God intended me to be. I can now go out and supply the fruit He has planned for me all along, for the secret was for me to not feel like I did not fit in anywhere but that I always fit into His kingdom. All God sees is completeness in my incompleteness, a true healer.

Feed the hungry, and help those in trouble. Then your light will shine out from the darkness, and the darkness around you will be as bright as noon.
                                        —Isaiah 58:10 NLT

CHAPTER 16

Precious to Him

I am identical to the leaf breaking free and gently gliding from the branch in the wind for now I can see that it Is all connected to the calling of the Lord. It resembles a flower that is elegantly different in colors, sizes, and shapes yet so unique and cherished. The things of nature are precious to Him and so am I. Without a thought, He gives so much to the world, not just in beauty but in supplying food for insects and animals. He was preparing me prophetically for the space He was creating for my growth. I, too, am complete. Not one is more beautiful than the other. The world is made up of those who are complete and who are incomplete, but the truth of the world is that we all are extraordinarily magnificent and created with intention.

What the heavenly Lord let me witness while being in a coma was not impressionable in comparison to the magnitude of His love for us. His love is unconditional and pure and is not held back from anyone. The colors of my life are brighter, and I can see things clearer. His arms are open, I can run into them. Embracing the path God has planned all along helps me to discern that the heavenly Father was not punishing me. It was myself. Walking with the Father, I experienced the freedom I have been longing for. My past thought processes would think if I let God have all my power, then I will be letting someone have control over me. The actuality of surrendering control is to not let the spirit of fear and anxiety have power. Once I broke those chains and let in the love and light of the Lord, I felt the true freedom. God's unconditional love and grace, which He meant for me all along, continues to help me walk the path hand in hand with the Holy Spirit.

For other moms, dads, and loved ones who are feeling heavyhearted over someone sick or unreachable in their lives, I am writing this book. God wants me to let you know the love He has for the ones we hold so close to our hearts, which seems in a place of untouchable condition to us, is so richly consumed in laughter and joy, happiness, and safety. Please know there is a safety of embraced atmosphere of love surrounding them.

I am honored that God asked me to write my testimony and adventures through this world for His kingdom. There are no words in the dictionary that could come close in explanation to what my five-year-old self felt in those moments of the journey and appreciating that He gave me the opportunity to witness it again at forty-eight years old. There is an immense amount of heavenly love captivating one's soul with joy and light pouring out over us as a gift from the Lord that He freely seeks to give with no strings attached. It is His adoration of us that guides us to grow in intimacy together. If there is one prayer that I have for you after reading this book, it is to know that in the eyes of God, you are loved and complete.

*They shall neither hunger anymore nor thirst anymore;
the sun shall not strike them, nor any heat; for the
Lamb who is in the midst of the throne will shepherd
them and lead them to living fountains of waters. And
God will wipe away every tear from their eyes.*
—Revelation 7:16–17 NKJV

ACKNOWLEDGMENTS

I would first and foremost like to thank the heavenly Father who revealed to me through the power of dreams how much He loves me…then, now, and always. I thank the Holy Spirit who was right by my side as I wrote every word All the Glory Goes to God. I feel truly humbled and honored.

Thank you for your patience and kindness, Dennis Seeds, and his beautiful wife, Sue, who have gently supported me with your friendship and all the help with this book. I know there was no coincidence that God called Dennis to help me see a way at times when I could not.

For the love of my life here on this heavenly planet, I cannot thank God enough for putting David in my life. For being the most supportive husband and loving me through my good, bad, and ugly. I have watched God move mountains in our life and feel truly blessed that He put you for my spouse who would love me exactly the way I am. David, thank you for always making me laugh at myself and lightening my load. I love you.

My children, Julia and Steven, thank you for always being there loving me and calling me out on stuff even when I don't see it. It helps me grow. I am so proud of both of you. I love you beyond words and am grateful every day that God chose me to be your mom. You are incredible people with beautiful personalities. I can't wait to see where your future holds. Always remember God is walking before you and beside you. He is there for you, wherever you go in this life, and so am I.

Julia, thank you tremendously for all the times I knocked well bursting open your bedroom door to please help me make a chapter flow. Your tolerance with me to always stay serene and helpful amazes me, and I am so grateful.

Thank you to all my friends who have loved me and supported me through everything life must hold. You all are truly a blessing, and I couldn't have walked a day without you in my life.

To my sisters, I want to thank you for always stepping up and loving each other even through all our differences. May God bless and keep you, your families, and all the generations to come.

To King's Church Lakewood, Ohio. Thank you, everyone. You all hold so dear to my heart. My journey of faith has expanded beyond belief because of your openness to the heavenly Father.

I would like to thank the team at Christian Faith Publishing. I am so appreciative of all your direction and guidance through this whole process. I would especially like to thank Diane Giuffre, my literary agent, whom I felt an instant connection. Your exuberant joy and love of the Lord showed me where the Holy Spirit was guiding me.

This story is my truth as I remember it. Some dialogue was reconstructed for narrative purposes, but I have done my best to stay true to the facts of the events and to where the Holy Spirit was guiding me throughout this book. Others, of course, may have their own recollections or perceptions of events. Some of the names were changed for their own privacy.

The Lord bless you and keep you; The Lord make His face shine upon you, And be gracious to you; The Lord lift up His countenance upon you, And give you peace.
—Numbers 6:24–26 NKJV

APPENDIX

Encephalitis
noun | en·ceph·a·li·tis | /enˌsefəˈlīdəs/
Inflammation of the brain, caused by infection or an allergic reaction

Symptoms:
Confusion, agitation or hallucinations
Seizures
Loss of sensation or paralysis in areas of the face or body
Muscle weakness
Problems with speech or hearing
Loss of consciousness (including comma)

In infants and young children, signs and symptoms might also include the following:
Bulging in the soft spots (frontalis) of an infant's skull
Nausea and vomiting
Body stiffness
Poor feeding or not waking for a feeding

Irritability
Pathology—inflammation of the brain tissue

MENINGITIS
noun | men·in·gi·tis | /menən'jīdəs/
Inflammation of the fluid and membranes (meninges) surrounding your brain and spinal cord

Symptoms:
Sudden high fever
Stiff neck
Severe headache that seems different from normal
Headache with nausea or vomiting
Confusion of difficulty concentration
Seizures
Sleepiness
Difficulty waking
Sensitivity to light
No appetite or thirst
Skin rash (sometimes, such as in meningococcal meningitis)

In infants and young children, signs and symptoms might also include the following:

High fever
Constant crying
Excessive sleepiness or irritability
Difficulty waking from sleep
Inactivity or sluggishness

Not waking to eat
Poor feeding
Vomiting
Bulge in the soft spot on top of a baby's head (fontanel)
Stiffness in the body and neck

PNEUMONIA
noun | pneu·mo·nia | /n(y)oō'mōnyə/

Lung inflammation caused by bacterial or viral infection, in which the air sacs fill with pus and may become solid. Inflammation may affect both lungs (double pneumonia), one lung (single pneumonia), or only certain lobes (lobar pneumonia)

Symptoms:
Fever
Chills
Dehydration
Fatigue
Loss of appetite
Malaise
Clammy skin or sweating
Respiratory (fast breathing, shallow breathing, shortness of breath, and wheezing)
Also common: coughing or fast heart rate

HEPATITIS A
noun | hep·a·ti·tis A | /hepə'tīdis ā/

Highly contagious liver infection caused by hepatitis A virus. The virus is one of several types of hepatitis viruses that cause inflammation and affect your liver's ability to function

Symptoms:
Fatigue
Sudden nauseous and vomiting
Abdominal pain and discomfort, especially on the upper right side beneath your lower ribs (by your liver)
Clay-colored bowel movements
Loss of appetite
Low-grade fever
Dark urine
Joint pain
Yellowing of the skin and the whites of the eyes (jaundice)
Intense itching

TYPE I DIABETES
noun | type one di·a·be·tes | /ˈtīp-ˈwən-dahy-uh-bee-tis, -teez/

Once known as juvenile diabetes or insulin-dependent diabetes, is a chronic condition in which the pancreas produces little or no insulin. Insulin is a hormone needed to allow sugar (glucose) to enter cells to produce energy

Symptoms:
Increased thirst
Frequent urination

Bed-wetting in children who previously didn't wet the
bed during the night
Extreme hunger
Unintended weight loss
Irritability and other mood changes
Fatigue and weakness
Blurred vision

SUICIDE PREVENTION LIFELINE | 24-7
National Suicide Prevention Lifeline: https://suicidepre-
ventionlifeline.org

DEPRESSION HOTLINE | 24-7
Depression Helpline: https://www.mentalhelp.net

He heals the brokenhearted And binds up their wounds.
—Psalm 147:3 NKJV

BIBLIOGRAPHY

The Holy Bible:

English Standard Version (ESV):
Scripture quotations marked "ESV" are from the ESV Bible (The Holy Bible, English Standard Version), © 2001 by Crossway Bibles, a publishing ministry of Good News Publishers. Used by permission. All rights reserved.
http://www.crossway.org

New International Version:
Scripture quotations marked "NIV" are taken from the Holy Bible, New International Version®, NIV, © 1973, 1978, and 1984 by Biblica Inc.™
Used by permission of Zondervan. All rights reserved worldwide.
http://www.zondervan.com

New International Reader's Version:
Scripture quotations marked NIrV are taken from the Holy Bible, NEW INTERNATIONAL READER'S VERSION, ©

Book: *Mayo Clinic Family Health Book*, 5th Edition 2020
Book: *Mayo Clinic Guide to Raising a Healthy Child*, 2020
Book: *The Essential Diabetes Book*, 2021

The picture was taken 7 months after I got out
of the hospital and the year was 1977.

ABOUT THE AUTHOR

Michelle Strong is from Westlake, Ohio. She has two beautiful children, Julia and Steven, and a loving husband, David, never wanting to leave out her adorable dog, Q-tip, and her crazy cat, Kitten. She is a member of King's Church in Lakewood, Ohio.